ASK
for Success!

21 Ways to Enhance Your Image and Maximize Your Potential

by Gerry Reid

Edwin Thomas & Sons, Publishers

Flower Mound, Texas

Dedicated to the rock polisher.

4

∞

Appreciations and Acknowledgements

"There is no greater token of esteem, save one's life, than to generously give to another what one knows. Thank you, my friends, for your gifts."

— Gerry Reid

For as long as I can remember I have told people "Someday I'm going to publish a book." Someday has finally arrived.

No one writes or publishes a book alone. Even with hundreds and hundreds of hours spent apart from people, in front of the computer, with pen and paper, or in research, there is always the presence of those who love, encourage, support, teach, mentor and guide the author. I did not expect writing a book would be easy. It was not easy. One of the most difficult parts was writing this section.

While I talked about writing a book, others encouraged me to do it. While I dreamed about it, others provided real examples. While I searched for what it would contain, others gave me ideas and inspiration. While I thought about it, others lived it. For some reason, be it fate, a poor memory, or an over-active imagination, I am moved to directly thank the following:

Thank you Pam, for being my best friend, my wife, my lover, my counselor, my partner and my number one editor. Your lapidary skills are astounding. I am the most fortunate man on the face of this earth. I love you, Babe.

Thank you Mom and Dad, for writing to each other so faithfully. Books, letters and lives are written one page at a time, with passion and perseverance. In both of your cases life was unfair and unjustly short. Rest in peace.

Thank you Beverly, my sister, for the very real example of our not knowing how long we have. All I can say is P.P.B.M.G.D.S.H.A.F.

Thank you Roy Highland, my tour guide, wherever you are, for seeing something special in me. Little did you know back then how profoundly you shaped my desire to make something of my life and how important it is to enjoy living and to accept myself. "Husky" does.

Thank you Bill Kluckas, my surrogate dad. You recognized my leadership potential before anyone else did. The opportunity you gave me really paid off! Unfortunately, M,M,STMMARV. I'll have to settle for hind tit.

Thank you Bob Jamison, my life-long friend, for teaching me "When you've got the balls, you can go anywhere." Together we have looked at the stars, listened to the blues and felt the vibrations of friendship. These are the foundations of all great thought.

Thank you Hein van Steenis, my student, for showing me what impact I was having when I least knew it, and in The Netherlands, no less! Books written by ordinary folks like us, provide the example needed for the next blossoming author.

Thank you Danny Raphael, my follow-through role model, for demonstrating how nice it makes other people feel to be a gentle man, and a gentleman. If nice guys finish last, the pearly gates will have rusted away by the time you get there.

Thank you David Meier, my accelerated learning mentor. I love being your neighbor. You have such a nice neighborhood. Everything seems so real. That is probably why it works, don't you agree?

Thank you Gene Ciliberti, my delivery mentor, for helping me understand that I cannot "teach," for warning me about the person blocking my road and for being my launch director. The view from orbit is just as beautiful as you said it would be.

Thank you Dr. Michael Berger, my recursive coach, for helping me learn the importance of skill, knowledge, attitude and recursiveness. You gave me exactly what I needed to begin my journey: a kick in the ASK!

Thank you Trevor Perry, my upside-down friend, for your enthusiastic support and outstanding editorial assistance. I'll shout ya' a cold one next time we go a'waltzing.

Thank you BSers everywhere, my audience, for listening and participating; especially those who took the time to write. The next book is dedicated to you. This one is about you.

Thank you Jonathan and Jason, my honorable #1 and #2 sons. Because both of you have such quality and character, I have been able to spend more of my life growing rather than worrying. If all parents had children such as you, the social problems of this world would be gone forever. I could not be prouder!

In addition, Jonathan, thank you for the *Gerry Reid Speaking* logo, and Jason, for the concept of the cover of this book. My publisher, Edwin Thomas & Sons assures me they will publish your book, Jonathan, based on the research they have seen so far. Jason, your first art book is a guaranteed success because of your uniqueness and proven ability.

To all the other wonderful people who have influenced and encouraged me, those I have forgotten to mention, I can only say "I'm sorry, it was not intentional." The toner has been fused, the ink is dry, and the glue in the binding is set. I can no longer change it.

A special thank you goes to you, my reader. Your confidence in me is humbling. My hope and prayer is for you to find this book educational, helpful and inspirational. I am no different than you; no better, no worse. I simply chose this path to try to make a contribution. Your reward and my reward are the same. We have touched each other.

Finally, thank you God, my constant companion, for undeserved and untold blessings. Thank you especially for: Pam, Jonathan and Jason, your patience with me, the spirit to write, grace, peace, and forgiveness.

Gerry Reid

Gerry Reid - September, 1994

> "You cannot teach a person anything, you can only help them discover it from within."
>
> —Aristotle

ASK for Success!

21 Ways to Enhance Your Image and Maximize Your Potential

Table of Contents

Introduction

ASK for Success! will help you discover ways to expand and enhance the "people side" of your personal and professional life. Its objectives are:

- ▸ **To challenge you** to project more energy and enthusiasm about people.
- ▸ **To empower you** to become a more significant contributor to the organizations and people you serve.
- ▸ **To enable you** to obtain more personal self-satisfaction.

The aim of *ASK for Success!* is to provide reasonable, simple, and easy-to-use techniques and strategies to answer these three questions:

- ▸ What can a person do to help **reduce negative stereotypes** of their profession?
- ▸ What characteristics help **enhance professional image?**
- ▸ What are some ways to **discover, nurture and increase personal potential?**

ASK for Success! is a collection of ideas, tidbits, to-do's and philosophy collected over a lifetime in the business world. I make no claim to have mastered all the ideas presented here. I have tried them all and they work for me, some better than others, and those probably due to repeated use.

Some topics in this book may seem like common sense; others will be new to you. Applying any or all of the concepts described in these chapters will build and encourage the positive aspects of your personal self-image.

To qualify for inclusion in this collection, a topic is one of the following:

- ▸ Things I have tried and found to be beneficial in my personal or professional growth.

- ▸ Something I wish I had paid more attention to or had done earlier in my life.

- ▸ Ideas suggested by business and personal acquaintances that made significant and immediate improvements to this book.

- ▸ Items that are part of my current to-do list as I look for new and improved ways to discover the secrets of highly successful, technical professionals.

I sincerely believe by doing some or all of the ideas and techniques presented here, you will, with dedication and practice, increase your value to your employer, other people, and your personal sense of self-worth.

If, as a result of reading this book, you do just one thing differently, and become prouder of who you are or more satisfied with your contribution, then we both will have succeeded.

Before you dive into Part I, I'd like to describe a few things about my writing style.

Since this is my first book, my style is not yet established. You might say "Gerry has no style!" (But please don't! :-) I have attempted to write in an informal, conversational way. It is my hope while you read this book, you will feel as if you and I are sitting somewhere in a very comfortable environment having a one-on-one discussion of the topic.

I tend to use "they" and "their" as singular pronouns, which I know will cause frustration for some readers. I think the "he/she," "s/he," "one's" and other ways of producing gender neutral terms have gotten completely out of hand. In my defense, I refer you to the latest Bulletin for Unisex Language Latitude in Social, Homogeneous and Intellectual Transactions[1] published by Edwin Thomas & Sons.

Grammar checkers tell me I have been using too many passive sentences, (I guess I'm just a passive kind of person ;-) I put commas where they don't belong, (my excuse is, it helps the reader "listen" to written inflection), and I sometimes place punctuation where it shouldn't be (because I like smiley faces and putting the punctuation

---

[1] The American Board of Correct Diction and English Formulations. They indicate a growing acceptance of the use of "they," "them" and "their" as singular, non-gender pronouns. A copy of the bulletin may be ordered from the publisher. See order form inside the back cover.

inside the parenthesis may change the meaning of the face!-) Some of my infinitives are split, some overly complex sentences with many clauses are present, and I tend toward dangling an occasional participle, because English was one of those subjects in school I was not very good at or fond of.

I also like to put some expressiveness into the printed word through the use of *italics*, **bold**, CAPITALS, em-dashes — , quotation marks "", smiley faces :-) (a hold-over from my electronic mail habits) and other non-standard things I think will help you better understand what I am trying to say.

Clichés are included for those who do not like metaphors and would rather stay on top of things by taking personal responsibility for making a difference. Metaphors are included for those who would rather take personal responsibility for making a difference by staying on top of things.

Contractions and single-stroke quote marks (') are used once in a while 'cause I'd kinda' like this book to read in a similar way to how I talk; sorta' like a mix of inner-city Detroit up-bringing ("The 'hood at Mack and Gratiot"), 1960's middle-America suburbia (409's, Hemis, Porcupines, Dual-quads and Six-packs), seven years living in rural Minnesota ("Uff-da, dat vas a big Deere, ya' sure!"), CB radio ("Breaker, breaker, one-nine, Good-Buddy, c'mon back!") and nine years in the great state of Texas ("Y'all myte coud stop bi fur a Lone-Star an' sum brisk't nex' tyme yur ridin' thru. Wur rat-cheer waitin' fur ya'.")

The ideas presented in this book apply to all people, regardless of position, background, race, culture, sex, natural origins, etc. If you find exception to that premise, where I have slighted, overlooked, assumed or have otherwise been insensitive and you are personally offended in any way, I hope you will know such offense is purely unintentional and due to my own naïveté and ignorance. (As a society in general, I believe we have become much too sensitive to being sensitive, and if I'm being too insensitive about it, I'm sorry. In other ways we have become much too insensitive about being insensitive and if I'm being too sensitive, I'm also sorry. :-) Personally written apologies will be sent on request.

I encourage you to get involved with your copy of this book. The wide outer margin is intentional. Add your thoughts, comments or notes there. There is nothing as wonderful as picking up an old book to find not only the author's thoughts, but the thoughts of one or more of its readers. There will be some minor exercises for you to do. Be sure to do them. They are there to enhance your learning.

Finally, you will notice I include an occasional quotation or FFT (Food For Thought) in boxes like this:

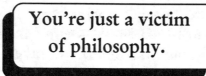

You're just a victim
of philosophy.

Every book, seminar, presentation and person I have encountered is fair game as a resource. If I can remember the source of a particular tidbit or quotation, it will be so noted. (As one gets older, the second thing to stop working is the memory — I forgot what the first thing was.) If you know of the original source for any of the information presented, please let me know what you know so there will be proper acknowledgement in later editions.

If you find errors, misquotes, violations of desktop publishing standards, or other distractions my editors and I have overlooked, please send me a note about it. Use the address on the copyright page or on the order form inside the back cover. The only way I will improve is to have the opportunity to consider your perspective.

Above and beyond all these reasons, I simply would love to hear from you personally. A letter from you would make my day a special one!

Let us begin . . .

PART I

The Foundations of Success:

Pride and Acceptance

Pride in Your Specialization.

Every job, no matter what it is, has its technical aspects. Technology is not just electronic and mechanical things. It can be the procedures, rules and regulations and "how-to's" of daily business activities. The specialization you bring to your job is your "technical expertise." This expertise may be how to sort the mail, which seasoning is needed to enhance a meal, what level of exposure will get the proper x-ray, when is the best time to run the system backup, why the wing flaps must be set at 20° — the list can go on and on!

People who have strong human-to-human skills balanced with technical expertise are called leaders, masters, consultants and influencers. They are considered to be assets to their employers. People with similar technical competence, but with little regard for people skills, are stereotyped in negative ways. These negative images lead people to think a technician, unable to deal with people, is a liability rather than an asset. Since every business wants to reduce its liabilities, some people find their jobs, and their careers, at risk.

Our specialization and technology are both assets and liabilities. The assets are the wonderful things made possible, better, easier and more productive through our skills as technical experts. The liabilities are in the negative images created about the technical person.

Technical people are well aware of the negative image given them by others in the non-technical community. Clients, customers and users of our services see us dressed in white lab coats, or wearing green visors, or having pockets bulging with pens and templates, or hands covered with grease, or arms full of manuals, diskettes, calculators and folded paper on which is printed strange languages, symbols and numbers. Behind our backs they call us "Nerds," "Bean-counters," "Bureaucrats," "Bit-twiddlers," even "Geeks." On the other hand, we tend to use that very word to describe ourselves.

— A short background story. —

At a recent meeting of COMMON[2], I conducted a session on creativity where I asked the 145 people in attendance to generate a description of themselves using words starting with the letters C, O, M, M, O, N. Over 60% of the participants chose "Nerd" as the "N-word." Asked if that was a negative image, the audience's response was "Yes."

Later that day I was in a planning session for the next COMMON meeting. Based on my observations during the creativity session, I said I

---

[2] COMMON is an association of IBM mid-range computer users.

---

would develop a new presentation titled "Nerds are People, Too!" The conference planner said, "You can't call our members Nerds!"

My response was, "Well, that's what they call themselves!" He said, "It's OK for them to call themselves Nerds, but it is <u>not</u> OK for other people to call technical people Nerds. It would be taken as an insult."

As a result of his advice, a presentation titled *Techies are People, Too!* was born. From that speech came the beginnings of this book. During the time I was researching and writing, I was also giving motivational speeches based on its content. No less than five audience members commented, "I hate it when people call me a Techie, I'd rather be called a Nerd!" Since I believe what Abe Lincoln said, "You can't please all the people all the time," I changed the title to *ASK for Success!*

— End of story. —

How can we get rid of or reduce these negative stereotypes? We can start by becoming more aware of what successful people do to create and maintain positive personal and professional images.

I have met thousands of technical people in my career as a computer programmer, engineering systems analyst, technical manager, technical marketing support representative, senior instructor and professional speaker. My peers and mentors taught me the importance of study beyond the technology and specialties of our jobs. To assure our success, we must study, understand and practice ways for adding value to ourselves and value to our businesses. We need to maintain our technical competence, put more emphasis on the people side of the business, and enhance our professional image.

Successful technical professionals maintain a high level of competence in both technical *and* people abilities. They are consciously aware of their abilities in terms of their attitudes, skills and knowledge. They study and learn the latest techniques and methodologies of their job. They also continuously explore and acquire new ways for communicating and dealing with people. Successful technical professionals believe in life-long learning.

Much too often, technologists bury themselves in learning only about technology. The result is a tremendous collection of technical information and abilities but little in the area of the attitudes, skills and knowledge necessary to help others.

> **When we fail to successfully deal with the people side of the business, we diminish our personal, technical and professional potential.**

I frequently give personal and professional development presentations to conventions, conferences, business meetings and leadership classes. What I have observed is, without exception, the most successful and most highly respected technologists are eager to learn about "people" skills. They actively seek information on how to grow personally and professionally. They recognize non-technical skills as the most difficult to master, the most difficult to quantify, yet the most rewarding to possess.

The who, what, where, when, why and how of business is of virtually no use if we cannot successfully communicate that information to others. Technologists who arrogantly use insider jargon, who project an image of superiority and who are insensitive to the perceptions and relationships of other people, limit their contribution to the business.

On the other hand, technologists who are sensitive, respectful, self-assured and sincerely concerned with communicating in understandable ways, find success is a satisfying by-product of professional behavior. These people become masters of human relationships as well as masters of their technology and they form productive partnerships easily. As a result, they have a much greater value to their companies, the people they serve, and themselves.

While this book presents many ideas, tips and techniques, there is no one technique that will open the door to effective "people" interactions. In fact, many of the topics covered in this book are indirect in their ability to alter your ability to be a stronger "people" person. What is certain, is that when many seemingly minor techniques come together with practice and determination, the result is a major improvement in the overall image projected.

The most successful technologists universally agree — without their ability to communicate with the "users" of their services and technology, there *is* no service or technology. Success is a state of personal achievement dependent on both technology *and* people. A person's greatest success occurs only when attitudes, skills and knowledge from both the world of people and the world of technology come together in harmony.

The best way to begin your journey on the road to success is to . . .

Accept Yourself as You Are.[3]

In the P.S. of the introduction I described my writing style. As my style developed, I did my best to apply the most important concept of successful self development I ever learned — accept yourself as you are.

The one thing I hope you will take away from the P.S. in the introduction is the first major point in getting rid of the negative images people create for themselves. Personally, I find the following principle one of the most challenging to fully embrace and the most rewarding when it happens naturally:

> **Accepting yourself the way you are is the first step on the path to improving the way you will be.**

---

[3] And others as they are.

None of us are perfect. Hmmm . . .
None of us is perfect. Hmmm . . .

(Since I can't figure out which way to say it, I guess that proves the point about me and so I just start this way . . .)

We all have flaws.
If a person denies a flaw, they cannot get rid of it, since through the denial, it does not exist. If one can accept their flaws and admit the flaws exist, then, and only then, can one work on getting rid of or correcting the flaws.

The things we do accept about ourselves, those things we are most proud of, are the very things we become most sensitive about. For example:

My name is Gerald Edwin Reid. I am a white (Caucasian), male (heterosexual), 50 year old (AARP member), Lutheran (ELCA), and basically a Republican (very liberal). My hair is thinning and graying. I was born in Detroit and grew up in Berkley, Michigan. I am a descendant of German (Janusch) and Scottish (clan Donnachaidh, family Robertson) immigrants to the United States. I am a U.S. citizen by birth. I am confused why I can call myself a native Michigander, but not a native American.

One of my more extreme opinions is I think we have a global society in need of major change.

We need to be shaken up a bit and "get humble" in our relationship to the earth and the universe. A natural, dramatic global event (asteroid impact, solar flare, extraterrestrial invasion) might be enough to wake us up.

Now, I could take the position of being greatly offended if you assume "Gerry" is female only, or white means "Archie Bunker," or male means "chauvinist," or 50 means "over the hill." I could easily be put off if you think I am too opinionated. (I am, but that is irrelevant. ;-)

If we take offense at every perspective not exactly matching our own, we spend most our lives focusing on what we think is wrong about the viewpoint of other people. It would be far healthier and more productive for us to increase our level of acceptance of other people and their perspectives. If we were not different, we could not be individually unique. Through our uniqueness we find the beautiful diversity needed for synergy, teamwork and corporate success.

A short diversion.

"Are you a PC person? In this day and age there are people who will tell you that you must be a PC person to have any chance of being respected, acknowledged and accepted. Authors especially must be PC people to have any hope of being published and successful. Certainly, it is guaranteed, without PC competence one is extremely vulnerable to the anger of those who are PC people. PC people are most definitely on the lookout for those who are not PC people."

If you are a bit confused by the previous quotation, that's OK. The letters PC can mean more than Personal Computer (or Pocket Change, Presidential Candidate, Professional Crap-shooter or Professor of Chemistry). In the quotation above, PC means "Politically Correct." Re-read the paragraph, and this time substitute "Politically Correct" for each occurrence of PC.

My personal definition of Politically Correct is: being reasonably sensitive to those things making up our personal identity. Based on that definition I will say . . .

"This author, whose intent is to be PC, wrote this book on a PC. He suggests another PC person should write PC checking software for PCs. The author of this fantastic new software could be male or female, straight or gay, black, brown, red, white, yellow, old, young, urban, rural, white-collar or blue-collar, Christian, Jew, Moslem, atheist, Native-, Anglo-, African-, or whatever-American, abled, disabled, rich, poor, or any other personally sensitive issue that comes to mind."

By the way, this person, the author of PCPCPC (Personal Computer Politically Correct Pronoun

Checker), is **Attiskilkno** (at-uh-skill'-no), the most diverse person on earth, who, having a very complex family tree, has all of the characteristics mentioned.

End of diversion.

Personally, this concept of self-acceptance and non-judgmental acceptance of other people is one of the greatest challenges in my own life. The more research I do and the more writing I accomplish, the more I realize this is the greatest challenge you and I will ever face.

Many people would say the ultimate dream of humankind is peace in the universe, peace on earth and peace of mind. It is a cliché, I know, but everything starts with the individual: First me, then you, then everybody else.

If you adopt the principle that accepting yourself and the perspective of others is fundamental to personal growth, you are well on your way to getting the most value from this book. As for me, I continue to work on this issue in my life. I will most definitely have it mastered before my 200th birthday, how about you?

When people "lighten-up" on each other and begin a sincere effort to embrace the wonderful diversity of others, they instantly recognize the uniqueness of their own potential. These people quickly come to understand that only *they* can contribute the distinctive set of experiences and learning which built their perspective.

Furthermore, these people understand and accept the following FFT (Fhilosopy For Thought, hereby renamed from the earlier definition as a tribute to those readers who truly accept the author as he is) —

> **At this instant, the universe is exactly the way it should be. If it were supposed to be otherwise, it would be.**

What you have done with your life, right up to this very moment in time, is exactly what it should be. You cannot change the past; it simply was what it was.

Does this philosophy give you an excuse to sit on your butt and do nothing? NO! We must accept the past for what it is — the past. At this moment, the "now," we are challenged not to simply let the future become whatever other people want it to be, but rather to take an active role in shaping the future into the best possible future for us all.

The past is gone. The future is yet to be. The "now" is the only chance we have to influence the potential that our future will offer. The future will arrive, "just as it should be." But, what *should* it be? It is up to you.

Someone, this very instant, is doing something that will determine what your future holds. If that someone is not you, you are at the mercy and whim of every person who takes an active role in shaping the future. What if they desire a future of dominance, dictatorship or oppression (Attila the Hun, Caesar, Hitler, etc.)? You will be caught up in the flow of *their* future unless you take personal responsibility for *your* future.

What you become in the remaining moments of your life depends on what you do with what you have experienced, what others offer you now, and what you are willing to accept as your own responsibility. What you do to help others and what you choose to contribute to the system of life overall is entirely up to you.

If you can dream it, it can be.
You can dream new perspectives never dreamed by anyone else. You can open doors to ideas never thought by anyone else. You can discover things never imagined by anyone else. If you don't do it, no one else will, because they can't. As was sung in Andrew Lloyd Webber's smash London musical, "Starlight Express" —

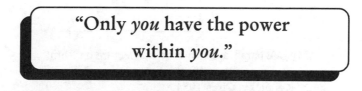

"Only *you* have the power within *you*."

The potential of the future rests on everyone's shoulders. Each of us has an undetermined effect on all others. There is no way to know if there is percolating in you the beginnings of an idea that will blossom into something to significantly improve the human condition. If you sign-off, and give up on your efforts to become all you are capable of becoming, you are the limiting factor for us all.[4]

Imagine if each of the following people did not pursue their grandest dreams. Certainly, the world would have not realized its current potential and would have been forever limited.

Moses	Abraham Lincoln
Caesar	Einstein
St. Paul	Salk
Joan of Arc	Gandhi
Galileo	Winston Churchill
Newton	Sister Theresa
Columbus	Martin Luther King, Jr.
Thomas Jefferson	Your grandparents
George Washington	Your parents

(This is obviously only a few of the hundreds and thousands of leaders who became significant contributors to your destiny.)

---

[4] My one paragraph synopsis of a lecture on Rural Sociology by Professor Pearly Acres, Burea College, Burea, Kentucky, Circa 1954.

Your potential, my potential, is no less than any other person, whether famous or unknown; rich or poor.

> # We have no way of knowing our limits. We have many ways to limit our knowing.

As you make your choices in life, when you choose to say "That's good enough." or "That's not my job." or "I've done all I'm going to do." you limit your own potential, *and* the potential of others. Your potential is no more than a dream, until you pursue it and turn it into reality.

Who knows the end result of your growth. Let's say you learn a better way to help someone use a new procedure or system. As a result they have a better day. The better day makes them less stressed and less tired. They are more alert on their way home. Their improved alertness allows them to notice a ball rolling into the street. They stop their car just in time to avoid hitting a young child. The child grows up to be a doctor. The doctor finds a cure for cancer <u>and</u> AIDS.

Far fetched? We have no way of determining our impact on the future or exactly what our potential is. We are like a seed planted in the ground —

> Our responsibility is not to be concerned with what we will become; our responsibility is simply to become it.

Each of us contributes to the overall picture of life. Any one of us, giving up and doing less than we know we can do, causes the picture to be less than it could have been. No matter what it is you hold within you, whether a unique color, texture, or brush stroke — without your contribution, the picture is guaranteed to turn out to be less.

> "Every action of our lives touches on some chord that will vibrate in eternity."
> — Edwin Hubbel Chapin

Every successful person I have met displays pride in what they accomplish and accepts the responsibility of contributing everything they can, for the good of all. To begin the process of contribution, these successful people first examine their current attitudes, skills and knowledge. They then learn what attitudes, skills and knowledge are needed to succeed. Finally, they seek ways to fill the gaps between what they have and what they need. The best way to start this exploration is to identify the elements of success . . .

PART II

Five of the Six Elements of Success

ASK for Support.

Attitudes, Skills, Knowledge. These are the three ingredients necessary to accomplishing anything. The letters they start with spell the word "ask."

To learn, we must ask. To ask means to inquire or to request information. We ask "Why," "How" and "What" to learn attitudes, skills and knowledge, the *ASK* elements. (For the remainder of this book I will use the symbolic representation *ASK* to mean "attitudes, skills and knowledge," and will refer to the three as the *ASK* elements.)

An attitude answers the question "Why do something?" A skill is an answer to "How do you do it?" Knowledge answers the question "What should be done?"

In school and college we learn knowledge. In trade schools and on-the-job we learn skills. In our life experience we learn attitudes.

My personal definition of **knowledge:** "comprehension and understanding of facts and ideas gained through observation, experience, discovery or study." The diplomas and certificates we so proudly display are symbolic of the knowledge we possess. These diplomas state that we are "qualified experts" in a particular subject area. Our knowledge is our resource. It is the library of information we have learned. It is available to us when needed. We go to this library to find out *what to do* as situations occur in our daily living.

When we gain knowledge it may be narrowly focused in understanding the depth and details of a given subject. Knowledge may also be a broad understanding of many subjects. Until we begin to ask "What do I do with what I know?" or "How do I do it?" we are dealing only with knowledge.

Skill is a "proficiency, facility, or dexterity that is acquired or developed through training or experience."[5] Our skill is the capability to do something productive; the ability to earn a paycheck. The things we do every day, whether on our job, around the house, in sports, or as part of a hobby, are the skills we have learned. Skills are at the heart of *how to do* something.

Of the three *ASK* elements, **attitude** has the broadest definition: "A state of mind or a feeling; disposition."[5] Attitude is most vulnerable to the judgment, perception and differing experiences of others. The attitude we choose motivates us, stimulates us, and provides the answer to the question of *why do it.* Of the three, attitude is the most difficult to learn because there are only opinions as to what is the "right" attitude to have at any given moment.

When stress rises under the pressure to perform, attitude is the first of the three *ASK*

---

[5] The American Heritage Dictionary, Third Edition

elements to be abandoned. Without the proper attitude, we stand a great chance of our skills and knowledge being rejected along with the rejection of our "bad attitude."

Each of us bring *ASK* to all aspects of our lives. Without all three in place and an even distribution of our energy among them, we limit our ability to achieve success.

The smartest scholar knows all about a subject. Outstanding technologists create wonderful new ways of doing things. A positive thinker can generate a fired-up and enthusiastic perspective. Yet, individually, each of these three lack the other two critical components needed to accomplish the overall task of getting the **whole** job done.

With just **attitude and skill,** a person has the will and the talent, but does not know what to do.

With just **skill and knowledge**, a person understands what to do and how to do it, but does not have the will power or the drive to begin, let alone complete the task.

With just **knowledge and attitude,** good intention and the wealth of information about what to do just sits idle without the skill to actually do it.

For success we need all three: **attitude, skill and knowledge.**

An *ASK* metaphor.

It is one thing to know what a right angle is, and something else to be able to cut a piece of paper at a right angle. To make the proper cut one has to know ways to make paper into different shapes. From our schooling (education) we know "what to do" to reshape paper into different shapes. We might cut the paper, tear it, fold it, wrinkle it, nibble on it, even take a laser beam to it.

The "how to do it" questions introduce the need for skills. Skills are many times quite mechanical. With training, we learn to use a ruler, square, pencil, scissors, and even a small knife. We are able to perform the skill to accomplish the task. Training (the learning of skill) prepares us for physical and mental processes. With practice, skills become sharpened and we gain improved precision and speed.

Without the third element, attitude, we would not yet have made a change to the paper. The attitude component supplies the "why do it" of our actions. "What is your motivation?" asks the director, psychologist, or self. We have something in mind as to what the reshaping of the paper will accomplish. It may be to create a tent card to display our name or fold a paper airplane that will fly. If there is sufficient reward for the action, we have an attitude (motivation) that empowers us to apply our knowledge and skill to do the work. In this example, someone reading our name off the tent card and saying it out loud, or our airplane flying the farthest or most gracefully may be reward enough to motivate us to action.

The importance of attitude.

Our attitude is learned through experimentation and adaptation of the behaviors of our role models. Most of the time our attitude is simply a habit.

We all know people who always seem to have a positive attitude no matter what situation they are in. There are also those who seem to find the negatives in everything they experience.

If the proper attitude is present, our skills and knowledge can be successfully applied and the objective of the situation will be achieved.

> **The best attitude for any given situation is the one in full support of the skills and knowledge being applied.**

Our *ASK* support us in all we do. When all three elements are in place, and our energies are distributed evenly among them, there is no limit to what we can accomplish.

ASK People.

I'd like you to meet some people. Do you recognize any of them? They may work with you. See if any of your associates come to mind in the following descriptions of seven types of people: **Know Only, Skill Only, Attitude Only, Know Not, Skill Not, Attitude Not,** and **Gotitall Together.**

Three of these people come from the Only family. They live on a dead end street in a remote corner of Lackland, a small town near you. The three Onlys are each gifted with one of the *ASK* elements. Unfortunately, they have no abilities with the other two elements.

Know Only is the local expert on everything but cannot demonstrate how to use the encyclopedic knowledge they possess. Know Only will frequently remind others: "A lack of knowledge makes you inferior to me." Know Only tends to say things like "Let me tell you . . ." and "I don't think, I know!"

Skill Only seems to always be busy doing something, but cannot explain what the results are good for. Skill Only takes pride in doing things with more precision and accuracy than anyone else. The favorite phrases of Skill Only are, "If it ain't broke don't fix it.", "A job worth doing is worth doing well.", and "We've always done it this way."

Attitude Only always has a smile and will tell you, "All you need is the right attitude." When pressed for descriptions of exactly what should be done and how to do it, Attitude Only says things to the effect of "It's all in your head!", "Think positive!" and "Imagine the fantastic results!"

These three siblings make Mr. and Mrs. Only a little bit proud of their children. The three Only children tend to have a great deal of conflict with each other and people in general due to their narrow view of the many options life has to offer.

The Not family lives in a more affluent area of Lackland, near the freeway entrance to Successville. Their three children make Mr. and Mrs. Not quite proud. Each of their children lacks just one of the **✻ASK✻** elements:

Know Not has a good attitude, and is skilled, but has to be told what to do. **Know Not** needs *education* to learn and understand the knowledge needed to become a well balanced contributor.

Skill Not has the right attitude and a wealth of information, but does not know how to get the work completed. **Skill Not** needs *training* to gain and develop the skills needed to become a well balanced contributor.

Attitude Not knows the many options of what can be done and how to do each one of the options, but does not have the disposition or will to carry through. **Attitude Not** needs *motivation* to acquire the attitudes needed to be a well balanced contributor.

Note: Attitude Not is a special problem child. Both the characteristics of "negative attitude" and "apathetic attitude" are projected by Attitude Not. Both attitudes are unacceptable and result in, but certainly are not limited to, a negative or "I don't care" attitude about: people, their abilities, places, things, the value of the work being done, and anything else that comes to mind. The list is unlimited.

These first six individuals fall into subordinate positions because of poor attitudes, inadequate skills, lack of knowledge or a combination of those conditions.

Finally, we come to **Gotitall Together.**
Gotitall Together has several sisters and brothers
including March, Learn, Pull, Work, Explore,
Grow and the new baby, Achieve Success. They
are a happy family and are very proud and
supportive of each other. They live on Happy
Trail at the intersection of Productive Path in
Successville. On the job, Gotitall Together is a
pleasure to work with.

Gotitall Together has a balanced approach in
the use of *ASK*. Gotitall Together has
a positive attitude, is well skilled, and has
a wide range of knowledge. Gotitall
Together is aware of the *ASK* needed
to accomplish the goals of the business.
While not necessarily by position or title,
Gotitall Together is most likely a leader.

Note: Another important characteristic
of individuals like Gotitall Together is
that they consistently seek new
experiences and information to assure
themselves they are up to date on the
latest thinking, strategies and research
about *ASK*. Gotitall Together realizes
learning never stops and enjoys the
growth process both inside and outside
their field of specialization.

Having met this interesting group of characters ask yourself these questions:

- Are there situations you remember when you acted like one of the seven individuals described above?
- Which of the seven is most like you at work? at home? at a social gathering? right now?
- Which of the seven do you most want on your team?
- Which of the seven would you avoid hiring?
- Which of the seven working for a competitor, would give you an advantage over the competitor?

All seven people on our team will grow by exploring, experiencing and thinking about the attitudes, skills and knowledge held by those people we call "successful."

ASK for ability.

All of the ***ASK*** elements combine in different proportions to form "ability." Ability is:

> **"having power, skill, resources or qualifications."**[6]

Recalling from the beginning of the previous chapter:

- **Attitude** is our source of *power*. Our motivation forms our attitude and creates our state of mind.
- **Skill** is our *proficiency*. Our talent to do things is the result of our skills training.
- **Knowledge** is our *resource* and our *qualifications*. We access, on demand, this library of knowledge acquired through our education.

Allowing for a liberal substitution, our **ability** is

> **"having attitudes, skills, and knowledge."**

In other words, we apply our ability (***ASK***) to obtain our success. We *ASK for Success!*

Let's take one short side trip before moving on to the study of the relationships of the ***ASK*** elements.

---

[6] The Random House Dictionary of the English Language, Second edition, 1987

ASK, as in questioning.

ASK can also be interpreted in another way, similar to the journey you are taking by reading this book:

> Ask, and it will be given you.
>
> Seek and you will find.
>
> Knock and it will be opened to you.
>
> Matthew 7:7

"What is there to learn?"

Ask. When you go to seminars, listen to tapes and read books for growth, you ask for information. In asking other people, "What is there to learn?" you will be given ideas and leads to many other sources.

"What is suggested?"

Seek. By investing your time and money, you seek information contained in this book and other sources. You are looking for application of new ideas in your life. Asking "What is suggested?" will help you find answers to your individual challenges.

"How will I know what to use?"

Knock. When you knock, you are actually doing the things you are learning about. "Opening the door" is the beginning of understanding how new skills and attitudes affect change in your abilities and perspectives.

The most satisfied and successful technical people follow a pattern of asking, seeking and knocking. They ask questions to learn about the attitudes of peers, clients, customers and themselves. They seek skills to enhance their technical competence and professional relationships. Finally, they knock on the doors of those who know. They gain knowledge from their mentors and open new opportunities for themselves by being aware of the need for constant growth and enlightenment.

> For everyone who asks, receives.
> Anyone who seeks, finds. If only
> you will knock, the door will open.
>
> Matthew 7:8

The proper balance of attitudes, skills and knowledge creates the ability to achieve success.

ASK Relationships.

There is an important interrelationship among the *ASK* elements. While each of the three can be thought of as *independent* concepts, they are *dependent* on each other. For example, a person needs to "know" about attitudes and skills, needs to have "skills" to acquire knowledge and attitudes, and needs appropriate "attitudes" to be motivated to gain knowledge and skills.

Furthermore, the three *ASK* elements are *interdependent*. Each element contributes to enabling the other two to become fully effective. Each one requires both of the others in order to be fully effective itself. This "one for all, all for one" approach means placing equal value on all three elements and not letting any one of them fall behind the others.

When a person does not focus on all three *ASK* elements in an interdependent way, there is an uneven distribution of ability. This is caused by too great an emphasis being placed on only one or two of the three elements. A highly technical person may put more and more effort into knowledge and skill in trying to solve a business problem while overlooking the very attitudes causing the problem.

> **The greatest benefit from your attitudes, skills and knowledge is realized when all three are fully activated and valued equally.**

For us to learn more about the *ASK* needed for success, we turn to people who have greater abilities than we do. These people are the richest resource we have for our growth.

Instead of expending energy trying to find little tidbits of evidence to prove we are smarter than they (when deep down inside we *know* they are smarter) how about simply admitting they have something we do not? Certainly there was a day when they did not know what they know now. At some earlier point in time, they could not do very well what they now do with great skill. How do you suppose they obtained the smarts we admire, need or desire? They probably admitted their short comings and got on with their learning.

Mentors.[7]

The purpose for having mentors is threefold. Mentors give us practice in recognizing that there

---

[7] Also see chapter 16, Have a Support Network.

---

are other people who know more than we do,
who have greater skills than we do and project a
more positive and helpful attitude than we do.

> **When you realize someone is
> smarter than you are,
> learn from them.**

No matter if it is attitudes, skills or knowledge, if
you feel you need what they have, admit it, and
tell them of your admiration and need. Then let
them become your advisor and mentor rather than
your adversary and nemesis.

Isn't it interesting — Sometimes the **only**
reason a person knows what they know, is because
they were once willing to admit they did not
know. Had they not admitted their weakness in
the past they would have never gained their
strength of today!

As you build your relationship with those
who know more than you, you might be surprised
as to the number of abilities **you have** that they
may want or need. The end result is one of mutual
admiration, camaraderie and synergy to
accomplish together what neither of you could
accomplish separately.

Knowing About Knowing.

Fools <u>do not know</u>
    that they <u>do not know</u>;
They just drift along
    with the same status-quo.

Sleepers <u>don't know</u>
    that they really <u>do know</u>;
Upon waking them up,
    they're ready to go.

Students and learners
    <u>know</u> they <u>don't know</u>;
Teach them and help them,
    then watch how they glow.

The wisest of all
    <u>know</u> that they k<u>now</u>;
Follow these masters;
    forever you'll grow! [8]

— Gerry Reid

---

[8] Based on an ancient Persian poem.

What is it the people in this poem know or don't know? It is *their ability*, and *their awareness of their ability* regarding their ***ASK***.

The individuals in the poem on the previous page are assigned several stereotypes. The following chart lists some of the words we may use to describe these different people. See if some of the names are those you tend to use to describe other people.

		Awareness of Ability	
		Unaware	Aware
Ability	Unable	Fool Unconscious Ignorant Unenlightened Backward Dolt Dumb	Student Learner Novice Follower Apprentice Mentee Pupil
	Able	Asleep Unconscious Comatose Stupid Distracted Forgetful Intuitive	Wise Conscious Cognizant Leader Teacher Mentor Master

With one exception (Intuitive), I would like people to associate me with the right-hand "Aware" column and especially the lower right "Aware and Able" corner. How about you?

Your potential.

Potential is defined as "capable of becoming."[9] When you learn, you increase your capability to become more than you were. Increasing your potential is a choice only you can make. You have to choose for yourself. By choosing to learn, you increase your potential.

When you are aware of both the abilities you possess, and the abilities you need, you can begin a program of growth. Your unlimited capacity to explore, learn and grow means your potential is unlimited too.

> **When you take advantage of every opportunity to learn, you maximize your potential.**

If you choose to take advantage of the information presented here and the associated possibility of growth, you will change and you will increase your potential. (Notice, I did not say you will increase your results. The results change only if you do something different than you do now. The results may be increased or decreased depending on how you measure them.)

---

[9] The Random House Dictionary of the English Language, Second edition, 1987

By reading this book, your potential is increasing. This is because when you finish, you will know more than you did before you started and you will have more options from which to choose as you make future decisions.

It is possible there is nothing new for you to learn in of this book. You may very well know everything presented here. If that turns out to be the case, I suggest you will still be changed, for many times a person's greatest learning occurs when they become *more aware* of that which they were already aware.

Even if you find nothing new, you will change and grow simply by the endorsement of knowing there is another person out there who thinks in a way similar to you. (If this turns out to be true, let me compliment you right now on how brilliant you are! Not many people would dare to admit they think like Gerry does! :-)

Balancing Your Abilities.

The major principle of this book:

> **Balancing "people" abilities and "technical" abilities is the one most powerful thing a person can do to realize their greatest potential.**

Many of the ideas presented in Part III of this book, *"Twenty-One Strategies for Success,"* are simple tidbits that influence the overall image projected by a technical professional. They all, in one form or another, point to the need of balance between "techie-do-ie" and "touchy-feely."

"Techie-do-ie."

A "Techie-do-ie" is a technically oriented person, one who has a job requiring a great understanding of detail, facts, procedures, terminology and technology. A technical specialist uses a unique language when speaking with people who understand the systems being discussed. Sometimes the jargon of these technologists gets in the way of successful communication with the people being helped by the technology.

The people who use the products and services created by the technologist are called the "end-user." The end-users are frequently overwhelmed when presented with the details of what goes on behind the doors of the department providing the service. Unfortunately, many times the technologist is so ingrained in the details of their knowledge of the systems used, they are unable to separate themselves from the procedures and technology. Thus, they are unable (or unwilling) to communicate intelligently with the very people they are trying to serve.

The result of such miscommunication is a negative and undesired stereotype about the technologist. They are seen as uncaring, unaware and unconcerned individuals. Unfortunately, the stereotype is sometimes well earned.

The finest technologists, the true leaders of the business in this high-tech, automated world, are those who can deal with the details and complexity of their expertise as well as successfully communicate with their clients and customers — the end-user. When technically competent people focus too strongly on the details of the technology, they are given negative labels as mentioned before. On the other hand, too great a concentration on the "people side" of the communication can produce similar undesired and negative stereotypes.

"Touchy-Feely."

People who believe successful communication needs *only* caring feelings, concern for others, and positive attitudes are sometimes referred to as "touchy-feely" types. They leave other people feeling they are "sucking-up," "manipulating," "beating around the bush," "full of hot air," or put into a name, an "Air-head." In this case, the technology getting in the way is the human technology of "people."

> **Successful technical professionals have mastered the attitudes, skills and knowledge necessary for dealing competently with other people.**

Competent technical professionals seek ways to keep their clients informed and *wanting* to learn rather than overwhelming the customer with information. Technical professionals know an overload of information causes the end-user to avoid essential communication with them. Such overload of information simply adds to the image problem. Successful technologists listen carefully to their customers and look for ways to fully develop abilities to deal with the concerns of other people. In doing so, they open-up their relationship with the world around them and discover their untapped and unlimited potential.

> ## Attitudes, skills and knowledge are <u>all</u> required to have success in balancing people and technical issues.

Imagine a circular plate, filled with bird seed, suspended by three cords attached to the edge of a round plate, one at 0°, one at 120° and one at 240°. The symmetry of such an arrangement makes a very stable platform. However, remove any cord and the contents will spill.

Imagine a second plate, suspended in a like manner, filled with the other requirement for the bird's survival — water. To survive, the bird needs both the water and the seed.

The *ASK* model proposes a triad to be kept in balance. The cords suspending our imaginary bird feeders represent attitudes, skills and knowledge. The bird seed represents the technical element of our job. The water represents the people element of our lives.

Like the seed, the technical content of our job nourishes us, gives us energy, and helps us grow as a result of our employment. However, we cannot survive, let alone succeed, with just food. Nor can we survive or succeed with just technology. We must have the refreshment and nourishment given us by people.

The interaction with people through communication, enthusiasm, and synergy is the support we need to accomplish our work effort. In our service to others, by helping their work become easier and more productive, our work is given purpose and meaning. Without water our body dies and without people the spirit of our success dies. To ensure our success, we need both food and water; technology and people.

The balance referred to in this chapter, and the entire book, may be thought of as the food in one plate and the water in the other. Both are needed for survival, health, strength and success. Likewise, we need a balance of technical and people abilities if we are to expect healthy, strong and successful job performance over time.

With corporate changes threatening every tradition of long-term employment, even survival itself is at stake. Without food *and* water, the bird dies. It is equally true of the technical professional. Without technical abilities *and* people abilities, the potential for success dies.

How success is measured is immaterial. For the bird it may be the need to sing its song, to be able to soar high above the ground, to defend its nest and territory, or to display its beauty. For the technologist, success may be the contribution made to a developing system, the pride in accomplishing something never done before, the satisfaction of isolating a failing element in a complex system, the receipt of a paycheck, or the recognition by others.

Having a balance between technical abilities and people abilities, plus symmetry among the *ASK* elements in support of them, provides us a much greater likelihood that our greatest potential is in place.

With our potential in place, we can begin to implement some specific behaviors leading to success . . .

Part III

Twenty-One
Strategies for Success

1. Give Others What You Demand in Them.

Using Table A on the next page, make a written list of ten characteristics you demand in the people you work with. Include things that come to mind when the other person is your peer, superior, subordinate, client, vendor, customer, or partner. Do not be concerned about what you think they want in you. **List what you demand of them.** Columns 1, 2 and 3 will be used later.

> Please participate in this exercise by actually writing in your book. It is very important to the success of your learning.

Table A

Characteristics I demand in the people I work with:	1	2	3
1			
2			
3			
4			
5			
6			
7			
8			
9			
10			

Go over your list. Make certain what you have listed is what *you* want in the people you work with. Please do not get ahead of this procedure. At this stage, *do not* be concerned about what they want in you.

Note how this list reads like a list of the most critical characteristics when hire, fire, promotion or layoff decisions are made. If the continued employment of those you work with depended on their performance in each of the ten areas you listed, how would each of them fare? Make a mental list of several of your associates. Who do you choose to be around and who do you avoid? If the time comes to lay people off, who should stay? Who should go?

A survey of 1024 people in attendance at my presentation *Techies are People, Too!* (story on pages 10-11) produced the information displayed in Table B on the next page.[10] In the table, the number in parentheses is the number of times the characteristic was mentioned.

> (Table B allows every person reading this book to have the opportunity to understand the result, even if some readers did not do the written exercise on the previous page. This, of course, does not apply to you. ;-)

---

[10] Complete survey results may be found in Appendix A.

Table B

Most Frequently Mentioned Characteristic
Demanded in Others:

Characteristic	1	2	3
1. Listening (88)			
2. Honesty (77)			
3. Humor (50)			
4. Respect (50)			
5. Friendliness (46)			
6. Non-technical language (44)			
7. Open-minded (36)			
8. Integrity (35)			
9. Positive attitude (34)			
10. Team player (33)			
11. Willingness to change (29)			
12. Communication (27)			
13. Dedication (27)			
14. Cooperation (21)			
15. Concern for others (19)			
16. Understanding (19)			
17. Knowledge (18)			
18. Courtesy (16)			
19. Skills (16)			
20. Compassion (15)			

In both Table A and Table B, let column 1 be labeled "Attitudes," column 2 "Skills," and column 3 "Knowledge." On each table place an "X" in the column that most closely identifies the nature of each of the characteristics listed. Do this now. (Please?)

For the vast majority of people, and virtually everyone surveyed, the number of Xs in the attitude column (1) far outweigh the number of Xs in the skills (2) or knowledge (3) columns. (It is interesting to note, the only reason there are 20 items displayed in Table B is that knowledge and skills of the job didn't show up until we get to the 17th and 19th most frequently mentioned characteristics!)

The nature of what we demand in others.
This exercise is *not* a study of what people demand in each other. It is a study of the *nature* of what we demand from others and what others demand from us.

We now have enough information to discover a powerful principle. What people demand from each other are *attitudes*. Skills and knowledge are important, of course, but they are not what is *most frequently demanded* by others.

The vast majority of characteristics we demand in other people are things reflecting a person's attitudes. Only if our attitude is right will people be interested in what we know and what we can do with what we know.

If we take the survey results to the extreme, we might conclude that skills and knowledge are of no use whatsoever without the appropriate attitude. However, taken in moderation, the evidence is overwhelming:

> **Skills and knowledge, while necessary and needed, are not the primary characteristics demanded by others.**

So, what is it we demand in other people even more than the skills and knowledge they bring to the job? Attitude. And what is it we should give to others on our journey to success?

> We must **listen**, be **honest**, have **humor**, give **respect**, be **friendly**, **speak with non-technical language**, and have an **open-mind**. We must do these things with **integrity** and a **positive attitude** about being a **team player** who is **willing to change** and **communicate**. Further we must do these things with **dedication**, **cooperation**, **concern**, and **understanding for others**. Then, and only then, are we asked to use our **knowledge** in a **courteous** way to apply our **skills** with **compassion**!

(Looks good, sounds good, and feels good, don't you think?)

This is *not* to say attitude is everything. There are days when the right skill or bit of knowledge may save the project. Even then, without the appropriate attitude, there is no access to that skill or bit of knowledge and, as a result, there can be no success. When the opposite is true, and there is no skill or knowledge available to save the day, then **only** attitude will have a chance to save the day — and in that case attitude is the **only** thing left.

Attitude can be of some value without skill or knowledge, but skill and knowledge are of no value without the appropriate attitude!

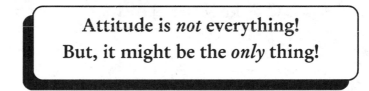

Attitude is *not* everything!
But, it might be the *only* thing!

Let's turn our thinking to this question:

What ✳ASK✳ do you suppose others want from you?

Think through this question from the other person's perspective. List what ✳ASK✳ you think they want from you in Table C on the next page. For each of their expectations, rate yourself in the "My Rating of Me" column. Then make a guess at what you think their rating of you might be in the "Their Rating of Me" column.

    Use a scale of 1 to 10:
        1 = Completely Unprepared
        10 = Fully Prepared.

Table C

ASK Others Want From Me:	My Rating of Me:	Their Rating of Me:
1		
2		
3		
4		
5		
6		
7		
8		

For every item listed, first compare your rating versus their rating. If the two do not match exactly, communication is needed to find out what must be done to bring your perspective in line with theirs. Once the two ratings match, if both ratings are not 10, there is still work to do. Answer these questions:

- Why are some of my ratings about myself not 10?
- What needs to be done to improve my rating of myself?
- What could I accomplish if my ratings of myself were all 10?
- Why do I believe some of their ratings of me might not be 10?
- What needs to be done to rate me a 10 from their perspective?
- What new gains could we make together if their ratings of me were all 10?

A Parable.

There is a new, delicious, healthy food in the world today. It is called a "Bit-O-Success."

> Now, the sad thing about a Bit-O-Success is that many people think it is not available in their area, supplies are limited, and it will cost too much even if they find it.

Yet, Bit-O-Success is unconditionally guaranteed to give you all the energy and enthusiasm you need for complete success. But, there is a catch. To be eligible to obtain a Bit-O-Success, you must first consume three other products to have a build-up of the proper nutrients before a Bit-O-Success is effective. One of the nutrients is found in a Bit-O-Knowledge, the Breakfast of Brilliant Brains.

> The most wonderful thing about a Bit-O-Knowledge is that you never know what is in it, until you open it.

But, you can't get a Bit-O-Knowledge open without the nutrient in Bit-O-Skill, the Snack of Smart Students.

> The most wonderful thing about Bit-O-Skill is that you never know what you can do with it, until you try it.

But, you can't try Bit-O-Skill without the final nutrient found in Bit-O-Attitude, the Appetizer of Able Achievers.

> The most wonderful thing about a Bit-O-Attitude is that you never know what you are capable of becoming without beginning to become it.

Now, here is the best kept secret in the industry — Every Bit-O-Attitude is free! There is an infinite supply available to everyone, everywhere, just for the asking. Also, Bit-O-Attitude comes complete with a lifetime supply of Bit-O-Skill and Bit-O-Knowledge! This means Bit-O-success is available in all areas, there is an inexhaustible supply and it costs nothing but a voluntary donation of your willingness.

As you enjoy the delicious taste of a Bit-O-Success, wouldn't you like to know how to get even more? The easiest way is to . . .

2. "Do It Yourself" and L.E.A.R.N.

I am always amazed when someone comes up to me after a presentation and says something to the effect, "That was interesting, Gerry, but what I want is a simple solution. Just give me a simple process to follow that will work in any situation. Tell me exactly what I should do."

Simple formulas and simple answers to complex issues produce only simple results. While some things in life can be reduced to "how to do it" equations, the results you can obtain from someone else's formula is limited. This book, or any other, offers only a minuscule subset of ideas and strategies that will form and empower your potential.

By definition, a "simple" solution will define something far less than your potential. While reading the following definition of "simple," from the American Heritage Dictionary, ask yourself if you really will be satisfied with a "simple" formula when developing your personal strategy for success.

sim·ple (s¹m"p...l) *adj.*

1. Having or composed of only one thing, element, or part.

2. Not involved or complicated; easy.

3. Being without additions or modifications.

4. Having little or no ornamentation; not embellished or adorned.

5. Not elaborate, elegant, or luxurious.

6. Having or manifesting little sense or intelligence; uneducated, ignorant, unworldly, unsophisticated, naive.

7. Not important or significant; trivial.

Sorry, I'll pass on the "simple" approach. What works for me may not work for you. What works for you may not work for me. I want solutions with options made just for me, even if it will take extra time and energy to obtain them. To excel, to be above average, and to continuously tap into and discover your potential,

> Find your own answers, create your own formulas.

There are many general principles that work for many different people. However, there is only one specific combination that will work for you. You have to research it, try it out, live it, and discover it yourself. Neither I nor anyone else can determine what you are to become.

> ## Learning about your potential and achieving it is your full-time job.

Adults cannot be taught. Adults *choose* to learn. Classes, seminars, audio and video tapes, educational television shows and books are available for you, an adult, to use in helping yourself learn. *You* choose to learn or not to learn. Learning is your responsibility.

Adult Learning.
Many years ago I developed a model of adult learning based on my experiences and observations as a facilitator and instructor. Adult learning is a five step process.

1. Listen.
The first step in learning is to listen. A considerable amount of what we learn is what we are told by others. We hear what they say. Listening also includes reading words written by

others, observing visual displays and illustrations, and sensing the feelings surrounding a situation. We listen to tone of voice, see body language and feel the emotions of the presenter.

Technical information is collected in the same way. We watch, hear and feel what is being shown, spoken and demonstrated. The internal conversation we may have with ourselves, even the handling of an object, is a form of listening. Taking something "in" is prerequisite to anything else happening, including learning.

> **Listening is the process of bringing information from the external world around us into the internal world of our brain and mind.**

All of this listening is one way — inbound. Effective listening in this step does not include judgment or comment. That comes later.

As we listen, we take the unedited information into our mind. Notice the symbolism of the word "information." We take something "in" and then let it "form" in our mind. This new presence takes on a "format" (either an attitude, a skill, or piece of knowledge) in the process of assembling into some usable "formation." Once we have listened to the world in this way, it is only then in the learning process we can express ourselves.

2. Express.

The word express at this point means to state our understanding of the information that has been taken in. Expressing is the process of rephrasing, reiterating what the presenter has said, or restating what we think we have heard, seen and felt. Expression can also be a statement of our initial reactions to the information.

To help the adult learning process it is important for an adult to express out loud, at least three things. First, an expression of what was seen, heard and felt. Second, an expression of how the new information relates to previous experience. Third, an expression of initial speculation as to what will happen as the new information is applied in the future.

> **When an adult expresses what has been learned, the quality of the learning is assured.**

By verifying the accuracy of what is now inside the mind, the adult learner can adjust their understanding before permanent, long-term learning takes place. If a learning experience is one with a live "instructor," this expression gives the instructor the chance to correct any misconceptions. If the learning environment is passive, as in reading, listening to a tape or watching a video, the expressing of what has been taken in will allow the learner to back up and review anything not clearly understood.

Relating past experiences and possible future uses is helpful in setting the new information into a permanent place in the mind. This process helps the learner remember new information by having something more familiar connected to it. The familiar, being easy to recall, brings the associated information with it.

Our initial reaction to new information is sometimes very revealing. The expression step is where those initial reactions occur. However, it is only in the next step where we come to grasp what was taken in as we "absorb" the information.

3. Absorb.

This step in adult learning is one of allowing the mind to take in and store the new information. Because of the extensive experiences of adults, there is a natural tendency to jump to a conclusion. This conclusion is a premature judgment and blocks the path to new learning.

> **Adults consciously processing new learning in terms of their experience must be aware of the tendency to prematurely judge and eliminate potentially valuable information.**

In the process of absorption, we need to consciously let information get past our disposition to reject new ideas.[11] We must work through the natural resistance we feel as we attempt to accept the new information. Our system may want to fight the new information, counteract it, and may want to deny it; therefore, this is an extremely important and conscious step. It is where we consider the new information over a period of time allowing ourselves to become accustomed to it. During this time the new information begins to reside more permanently in our mind.

Absorbing information takes time. Allowing information to remain available over a period of time gives multiple opportunities for the learner to find value and application. If information is prematurely judged to be of no value and, therefore, eliminated, there is obviously no chance of the learning being useful at a later date when our judgment of its value may be different. Being patient and consciously allowing time for our system to absorb new information ensures maximum benefit from adult learning.

Until we absorb the new information and have made it completely resident within us, we do not have the opportunity to do the following step, which is to reflect on it.

---

[11] See Chapter 19, Embrace Change

4. Reflect.

> To *reflect* is to determine whether information is applicable in a permanent way.

The process of reflection is where time is spent letting the new information potentially find a permanent place as one of our abilities. Many times, the opportunity to learn is denied way back in the listening or expression step; therefore, we sometimes eliminate ideas before they ever get a chance to come in and be reflected upon in light of all of our experience.

During the reflection step, new information is accessed many times. This accessing helps the information become more easily retrieved. The ongoing comparisons and connections with previous experience and projected uses puts the new information in perspective. This new perspective opens the door to the "Aha!" experience where the best use of the new information dawns on us and becomes obvious.

Once the reflection step is engaged, we may make a decision that this information is not of value to us and we may reject it at this time. Given that the new information had the opportunity to be accepted, the rejection in this step (rather than in an earlier step) becomes a much more mature (adult) process.

We start to look at the possibility of disagreeing with what we are learning, and at the same time understanding and accepting that this is the perfectly valid expression of another person. In other words, the other person has this particular viewpoint (the new information being considered), and believing the information to be true and useful, has expressed it. We begin to respect their perspective even if we do not adopt it as our own. The main benefit of getting to this step is in our becoming a better communicator. If we agree with their perspective, it means we are better at accepting the viewpoint of others.

Over time, by reflecting about the new information, we are able to categorize it and place it into our permanent, long-term memory. During the reflection process, we may come to the realization that this is good information. If we believe we need to use the new information in our lives, we accept it and allow it to begin the process of permanently altering our ***ASK*** and our perception. The final process in adult learning is the step in which we nurture our new abilities.

5. Nurture.

Nurturing means using the new information (be it attitude, skill or knowledge) often to learn even more about it. This last step is the one assuring us of completing the learning process.

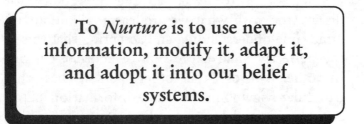

To *Nurture* is to use new information, modify it, adapt it, and adopt it into our belief systems.

Only through nurturing can new ideas and new concepts make us better people. For the rest of our lives we can use this new information.

At first we practice it. As we practice it, we get better at it. Nurturing goes on forever because no matter what *ASK* we have obtained, "If you don't use it, you will lose it." An old cliché, I know. Maybe this time we can more readily understand it and L.E.A.R.N. it.

Think back to some of the *ASK* you had several years ago. Chances are, those no longer needed are no longer nurtured. That makes sense. What you no longer need, you no longer use. And what happens? We lose the ability to perform those *ASK*.

If there are *ASK* that you need but seldom use, it is advisable to periodically project the image, flex the muscle or think through the thought pattern. In doing so, you guarantee yourself the resource is there when you need it.

```
┌─────────────────┐
│  Listen         │
│                 │
│  Express        │
│                 │
│  Absorb         │
│                 │
│  Reflect        │
│                 │
│  Nurture        │
└─────────────────┘
```

This learning process allows us to view another's perspective and then separately address the possibility of the perspective influencing our lives in a positive way. It should be noted, in this process there is no indication of teaching. There is no teaching being done by the other person. The other person is simply offering information for us to think about. It is up to us, as adults, to do our own learning — to seek the information we need and to find out what information is valuable to us. Then, having sought the new information, we must let it come into our system and change us.

A LEARNing challenge.

There was a book out about 20 years ago, title unknown, that said a person could become an expert on any subject if they spent just one hour per day for 30 days studying the subject. After 30 days of one hour a day study, a person would know more about that particular subject than 98% of the population. Studying for another 30 days, an hour a day, would make someone so much an expert on their particular subject they could probably write a book on it.

The point is, you can become an expert on just about anything simply by dedicating some time to learn the subject. So, if there is something you want to know about, research it, find out about it and study it.

Once you have learned something new, be it a new attitude, a master's skill or advanced knowledge, other people in need of the same *ASK* but lacking it, will come to you.

> **The more you learn, the more valuable you are to those who need, but do not have, your abilities.**

Now that you know the process of successful learning, it is a good idea to . . .

3. Educate Yourself — Study Outside Your Field.

When a person learns something new, there is an interesting side effect. For a short period of time, it becomes easier to learn *more* about subjects you already know much about.

Have you ever noticed the strange (and wonderful) feeling you get in your head when you learn something new? Personally, I find the feeling to be somewhat like the pleasure received when you do something nice for another person or when you have enjoyed a particularly entertaining evening.

Learning is addictive.

When your brain learns something, there is generated within it a certain chemistry causing permanent storage of the information. This chemistry is almost exactly the same as the chemistry produced when you have a "gut feeling" about something. Some theories go so far as to suggest the stomach (the "gut") is literally part of the thinking and learning system. Just like a gourmet meal satisfies the stomach, learning satisfies the brain. In any case, for me and for many people I have interviewed, learning something feels good!

I have noticed that when I learn something new, those feelings, or chemicals, hang around for a while. It is during the period of time after one event of learning we can easily learn other new information. If, while you are in this state of euphoric learning, you turn your focus to a subject you know, you will easily learn additional new information, building your expertise. This state of euphoria lasts anywhere from a few minutes to a few days, depending on the intensity of the "new" learning.

For example, when you have just learned something new (let's say something outside your field of expertise, like how to set the clock on your VCR), the "new" feeling generated in your brain is a result of the creation of the necessary conditions (chemistry) to learn. It is the ideal time to learn additional information about subjects you already know.

To frequently enjoy this physical pleasure of learning, we may have to do something as drastic as spend our own money on our education! Most likely we spent our own money to get our basic education and training in order to get to this point in life. Student loans, years of low wage employment while in school, driving the oldest and ugliest car on campus are all reminders of the personal financial investment made in our education and training.

Investing more in ourselves seems to be the obvious thing to do to advance even further. However, many technical people (mechanics, programmers, accountants, medical technicians, police, printers, etc.) expect their employer to pay for their technical education. If your employer demands you learn something new, there may be no option available to the employer and they must pay the bill.

Paying your own way.

What of the situation where *you* want to learn something you know will help your ability to do a better job, yet your *employer* does not have the ability or willingness to pay for what you want to learn? If you think you need to learn something to keep yourself technically competent, then by all means, seek the support of your employer in getting the education or training you need.

If your employer cannot or will not spend the money on your training or education, then approach the situation as follows:

1. Build a business case as to why this education will make you a more productive employee. Quantify your case. How many more things will you be able to do or generate in a given period of time with this new knowledge or enhanced skill? What does the new skill mean to current projects, specifications and deadlines? How might your new knowledge be transferred to your peers?

2. Diplomatically ask why you were turned down. If turned down, get an understanding of the real reasons for the lack of support. Is it the time away from the job? Is it the lack of a back-up person to fill in temporarily while you are gone? Is it the expense of tuition for the course you want to take? Is it the cost of travel and living expenses to the location of the class?

3. Negotiate to make this a win-win situation. Be willing to contribute some, or all of the time. This means sacrificing valuable vacation or holiday time in trade for your gain. If you have them, offer to use some of your frequent flyer miles or hotel awards. If your employer will give you the paid time, are you willing to pay some or all of the tuition or travel expenses?

4. Pay for it all yourself. The last option is for you to pay the tuition and expenses and take vacation time to get what you want and need. The extra value, determination and dedication you expend now may be rewarded at promotion time, salary increase time (or the lack of it at layoff time!) In any case, *you* have now acquired a greater asset *you* can offer to other potential employers and the opportunities they present.

In the meantime, what are your peers doing? Are they waiting for someone else to take responsibility for their advancement in learning and advancement on the job? Which employee would you rather have working for you — one who shows personal contribution and sacrifice during difficult times or one who just whines at the situation and expects the employer to foot the entire bill of making them smarter and wiser?

When it comes time to make the tough decisions about who goes, who stays, who gets promoted and who gets raises, I'm betting my management will remember the partnership I created through my self-education. And, if they don't? Well, there are a lot of other employers out there who just might want the knowledge I gained while I self-educated myself.

Inexpensive sources for learning.

Once you have committed yourself to this philosophy, your best deals on education are found in books, tapes, community education, public seminars and libraries.

Books.

Treat yourself to a new book, printed or recorded. You did that by obtaining this book. (Thank you! :-) How often should you get and read a new book? At least once a month. Preferably, more often. Even if you spend two hours pay per month on books, it is probably far less than what you spend frivolously. My guess is we all have at least one bad habit (smoking, fast-food, movie rentals, drinking, etc.) already costing us more than two hours pay per month. Trade the unproductive habit for one of growth and enrichment and you will be taking another step on your path to success.

You can double or triple your buying power on books and tapes by going to a half-price book store or by purchasing paperbacks. Even better deals can be found at flea markets, garage sales and auctions. Don't be concerned with the age of the book. Old books are filled with valuable and applicable ideas. Many current authors, myself included, are simply stating some basic principles in new words.

Don't overlook the current best sellers. Occasionally, very significant books have tremendous impact on our culture and those who are in the first batch of readers have a definite advantage over those who wait until everyone is talking about the "best seller." Examples of these significant titles include: *Future Shock, Megatrends, Seven Habits of Highly Effective People,* and *ASK for Success!* (Obviously, you know a classic culture changer when you see it!)

Local education.

Your local community is a excellent place to obtain inexpensive education. The evening courses offered through local colleges, businesses and civic groups are very reasonably priced and held in or near your community.

Watch your mail for public seminars coming to your city. Read the community, social and business sections of the local newspapers. In those sections you will find advertisements for local seminars and classes.

All of these sources will provide you with inexpensive ways to learn a variety of information related to your field of expertise. In addition, they are excellent sources to use when enhancing your more general abilities such as time management, creativity, interpersonal communication and the skills and knowledge needed in your hobbies.

Libraries.

The least expensive resource (free) is the public library. If you would rather not spend money, borrow books and tapes from your library. If they don't have what you want, request it — after all, it is **your** library. Call around. Most people have access to several community libraries, local university libraries, or on-line libraries. The resources are unlimited!

Hobbies.

One way to keep a mental balance between your technical expertise and the other non-technical aspects of your job is to have a hobby. It is valuable to have a hobby dealing with *ASK* not directly related to your job. Quite frequently, the skills of a hobby can be applied to issues at work, giving a fresh perspective. For example: the organizational discipline of stamp collecting applied to cataloging computer files, the symmetry and layout of a flower garden applied to the arrangement of tools in a work area, the safety awareness of woodworking or stained glass cutting applied to a construction site.

Workouts for your brain.

Think of your brain as a system of muscles. Let the different muscle groups represent the different subjects you know. Each individual muscle fiber represents a particular subject and the mass of the muscle is the depth or "strength" of your knowledge. Furthermore, let's say your technical knowledge is the right side of your body, and your non-technical knowledge is the left side of your body. With proper exercise, you become a well-balanced boxer, weight-lifter, body-builder, dancer, skater, swimmer, runner — whatever sport you choose.

Would athletes exercise only one side of their bodies? Of course not! Championship boxers with dynamite left hooks, need to have a good right-cross to have a balanced ability. Can you imagine body-builders competing with one side of their bodies looking like last year's world champion and the other side looking like a child? What would a figure skater be able to do with a strong and skilled left leg matched with an average right leg? Tennis players cannot be champions without both forehand and backhand ability.

What would happen to the weight lifter with the ability to lift 200 pounds with the right arm and only 100 pounds with the left? All of these images lack balance and performance would be lopsided to say the least!

Your professional potential is lopsided and imbalanced if you only exercise, develop and nourish your technical side. If your balance is off, you are vulnerable to stumbling and appearing out of control, and in reality, you are.

> **Your potential is more likely to be fully realized when you have well developed abilities in both technical *and* interpersonal areas.**

To learn even more about your personal side . . .

4. Keep a Journal.

If you will take just a few moments each day (as short as 30 seconds) you can create a journal that will help you get to know yourself better, will encourage and motivate you, and will provide a record of "you" for generations to come.

Journaling is very easy to do. There are no restrictions as to form or content. Journals can be private or public. They will always provide insight when reviewed at a later date.

The three rules of successful journaling.

Rule 1: Journal on a regular basis.
Regularity will help you make journaling a habit and will give you quality time with yourself and your innermost thoughts. Over time, regular journaling will give you results similar to regular physical exercise. Stress reduction, increased stamina and noticeable improvement in ability and agility are some of the life-changing and life-enhancing benefits of journaling.

Rule 2: Always date your journal entries.
Record the day of the week, the calendar date and the time of day. Occasionally, mention where the

journal is being written. This information will be of considerable help to historians reading your journal.

Rule 3: Do not criticize or critique your journal.

Journals are not meant to be literary masterpieces. Time and thoughts are lost if you demand perfection as you write in your journal. First and foremost, get your ideas written down. Then, only if absolutely necessary by your personal standards, correct errors, but most important, get it down! Your journals are somewhat like the notes you took in school. If you were required to hand your notes in, you probably rewrote them anyway, so it is best to let your journals exist exactly as you create them.

Journaling fundamentals.

A journal is not necessarily a diary, yet all diaries are journals. A journal is not necessarily a log book, yet all log books are journals. A journal takes on whatever form the author chooses. All personally written or recorded documents are journals: diaries, log books, histories, chronicles, notes, letters, memos, audio and video tapes.

Successful journaling takes place over many writing sessions. Each session need only be one phrase, sentence or thought. Recording more information in a given session enhances the breadth and depth of the thoughts recorded. Do not allow yourself to be discouraged by sessions producing only a few words. Discipline is the important factor. With practice and dedication, the thoughts will eventually flow naturally and rapidly.

Journals can be written in "blank books," in spiral tablets, on note cards, on calendars, on scraps of paper — virtually anything will do. Journals can be audio or video tape recordings. The medium is of little consequence. The value comes from the discipline of journaling and the product produced over time.

How did you acquire the habits you have today? Did they just start one morning, or was there a pattern of building over many weeks, months or years? Many questions about your habits and attitudes can be answered, at least in part, through the regular habit of journaling.

Keeping journals over long periods of time will help you see changes and rhythms in your life not observable in any other way. Once you examine your writings from a larger perspective, in this case, a longer period of time, you will see things that go unnoticed day to day and even month to month.

Journaling brings your behaviors into your consciousness on a regular basis. Healthy behaviors you observe can be accelerated into good habits by keeping the mind aware of the desired behavior. Similarly, bad habits can be avoided by seeing their patterns early and consciously eliminating the repeated behaviors contributing to them.

Let's try journaling, right now!

The remainder of this chapter will introduce you to several different forms of journaling. Get a pen or pencil and spontaneously write responses to the exercises on the next few pages. First of all, this will make your copy of this book unique to you and will help you gain a sense of ownership as you continue your study. Second, what you write today, if done with a serious attitude of growth and exploration, will become a beginning point. This will become the place where *you* started the changes that multiplied into your total success.

Spontaneously respond, in writing, to each of the following statements. As simple as this seems, it takes determination and commitment to actually **do** it. Ready? Set? Go!

Today is:

_____

The time is:

_____

Where are you?

_____

_____

_____

The weather is:

_____

How do you make a living?

_____

_____

What is the major news story of today?

_____

_____

_____

Where were you five years ago and what were you doing?

_____

_____

_____

_____

_____

_____

_____

_____

Describe a significant childhood memory:

_____

_____

_____

_____

_____

_____

If you could tell the entire world one thing, what would it be?

_____

_____

_____

_____

_____

_____

If you did this exercise, it is very likely you will remember much more than just those facts whenever you next see these pages, even years from now! One undeniable fact about journaling is when you write something down, you are far more likely to remember it than if you just think about it.

Even before you made these entries (You did the exercise didn't you? If you didn't, do it now!) you were already journaling in some form or another. Everything you write, be it reports, letters, memos, or post-it notes, they are all forms of journaling.

Journaling is an extremely powerful way to get to know more about yourself. The more you know of yourself, the better able you will be to determine what you want out of your career and out of life because you will discover patterns in yourself you cannot find or see in any other way.

To-Do-List Journaling.

The simplest form of journaling is to take a moment at the beginning of each day and write a to-do list. Writing a to-do list will help you visualize and focus on what you will accomplish today. As you think about the tasks at hand, you will find spontaneous thoughts occurring about the resources needed, the people involved, and the urgency of each item. Make note of these thoughts. They are the beginnings of the process of establishing how you will go about obtaining the additional information needed to get the work done.

Break complex tasks and projects down into manageable pieces. This will remove thoughts of being overwhelmed by the magnitude of the whole job. These smaller sub-tasks are also easier to delegate.

> ## Even the impossible becomes possible when broken into achievable tasks.

To-do lists also help in establishing ways to evaluate and measure the completeness of your tasks. As you record your list, describe what you will see, hear and feel when it is finished. These thoughts help your system establish the evidence to be measured that will determine the completeness of the task.

Examples:

"I will see the report bound in its dark blue cover with today's date and my name on it. I see my watch displaying 4:45 P.M."

"I will hear the silence as I turn my computer off and the voices of people telling me I did a good job."

"I will feel happy and proud, and will feel the warm hugs of my family as I arrive home at 6:00 P.M. sharp!"

Finally, this form of journaling will give you a reference point for determining the amount of progress made at the end of each day. Even if you just record your plan for the day, as long as you do it every day, your journal will become a log of what you planned to accomplish and a reminder of those things still to be done. To-do list journaling also gives an indication of the pattern of your thinking during the early part of your day.

What is it you need to do in the next 24 hours?

_____

_____

_____

_____

_____

_____

_____

_____

_____

What will you see, hear and feel to know you have completed each task?

_____

_____

_____

_____

_____

_____

_____

_____

_____

Noontime Journaling.

One unusual time to journal is at noon or lunch time. Most people think of journaling as a beginning or end of day activity. I have found the noon hour a great time to reflect on the progress of the day. If things are going well, this mid-day break reinforces the good feelings. If things are not going so well, this is an ideal time to regroup, forgive yourself for a bad start and rededicate your day to positive accomplishment. In both situations journaling is a way to log your progress and establish the best potential for the remaining time in the day. Noontime journaling is usable by both morning and afternoon people as it finds both of them near the time of their peak performance.

How has your day been so far? What is still to be done today?

_____

_____

_____

_____

_____

_____

Accomplishment Journaling.

This is the simple daily logging of your accomplishments. Make a note every time you complete something. As time goes on, you will start to recognize those things getting put off for long periods of time. This will clearly identify those things you may not like doing as well as the things you do not do very well. Examination of these items may reveal where you need to enhance your *ASK*.

At the end of the day, record all your accomplishments individually. Break them down to match the detail of your to-do list. Evaluate each item, and compliment yourself for what you did with this day, no matter how minor. Night owls will do well by journaling late in the day or just before retiring.

Regular use of Accomplishment Journaling makes those dreaded weekly and monthly reports a breeze. This form of journaling is also very helpful when creating justification for requested raises and promotions. Finally, your résumé can be created quickly and accurately by reviewing this journal.

Think back over the last few days and weeks. What have you accomplished in the last 24 hours? In the last seven days? In the last month? (If you are already into Accomplishment Journaling this exercise is easy!) Record you accomplishments on the next page:

_____

_____

_____

_____

_____

_____

_____

_____

_____

_____

_____

Dream Journaling.
(If you are the type of person who does not remember sleep dreams, use your daydreams, or call this section **Shower Journaling**, and use a white board and water-proof grease pencil in your shower and forget the tape recorder!)

Keeping a note pad and pen, or a small tape recorder by your bedside will serve two excellent purposes in your journaling. First, you will be able to record your dream events. Everyone knows the frustrating feeling of "I had a dream, and I know how I felt, but now I can't remember what it was about." or "I had a fantastic idea (solution, inspiration) but I can't remember it!" feeling. Journaling helps reduce the occurrence of such frustration and lost information. Second, a quick note upon waking will significantly improve your ability to gain from this creative time in your life.

Capturing your dreams and later attempting to interpret them or simply reflecting upon them is an extremely personal and private affair. Depending on your personal view of what dreams mean, your dream journal may give you a laugh, a tear, some inspiration, or a whole new purpose in life. Some experts say dreams are just random firing of neurons as we sleep, some think dreams are how we cope with stress, still others believe in metaphysical meanings and direct connections to other people, places, times and spirits. Personally,

I think all three apply at different times. (How's that for a cop-out? ;-)

There are a couple of drawbacks in dream journaling. Your partner may not appreciate the interruption of lights being turned on in the middle of the night, or a voice being recorded, and there is always the possibility of the following (true stories) happening to you:

> Being somewhat groggy when I wake up, I once found a dream journal entry in a scribbling I could not read! I guess I was half asleep when I wrote it down. I never did figure it out.

> The other extremely frustrating event was when I had a fantastic dream filled with revolutionary ideas and concepts. Things to make me rich, famous, happy and at peace with the universe. I awoke and wrote it down in exquisite detail. I did not want to repeat the "unreadable note" situation, so I carefully re-read my entry to verify it was not just scribbled gibberish, and went back to sleep.

> When I woke up in the morning, I found my note pad was blank! What had happened was I <u>dreamt</u> I woke up and I <u>dreamt</u> I wrote it down!

(By the way, I never made a journal entry about the last story. Somehow the irritation of losing the first dream forever was enough to permanently burn the event into my long term memory!)

What was the content of the last dream you remember? What do the images, sounds, feelings and events mean to you?

_____

_____

_____

_____

_____

_____

_____

_____

_____

Journaling while Driving?

Ideas sometimes jump out at us while we are driving. **Journaling while driving is just as dangerous as telephoning while driving, and I do not recommend either.** If you insist, the portable tape recorder or a phone call to your secretary, answering service or recording machine will serve to capture your thoughts of the moment. However, please be aware of the traumatic memory you may bequeath to a loved one or employee if you rear-end the gasoline tanker in front of you while leaving your message. (Imagine your loved ones coming home to <u>that</u> message on the answering machine!)

Journaling while Commuting.

Journaling while on a train, plane or ferry is great unless you are the engineer, pilot or captain.

Subject Journaling.

Another way to enjoy the benefits of journaling is to record all of the ideas and thoughts you have about a given subject. The topic doesn't matter. Choose something you think about frequently. Whenever you have a thought dealing with the subject, make a note of it in its special and separate journal. Over time you will have created a base of information containing a considerable amount of what you know and think about this particular subject. It can become a foundation for a book in your future or a place of reference where you know you can find all of the information you need about the subject.

ASK for Success! is the result of journaling for over 20 years, much of it on an irregular, undisciplined basis. I estimate I could have saved at least 30% of the time spent writing this book had I been more organized and disciplined about my journaling. In any case, I did capture a wealth of ideas and observations about a variety of professional development topics. This chapter was gleaned from several different journals and sets of notes. It would have been much easier if I simply had a journal about journaling.

My next book will be *Belief Systems: BS for All Occasions.*™ It is already in journal form. It will be a collection of word pairs starting with the letters **B** and **S**. The collection has inspired many Beautiful Stories to pop up in my Brain Soup. Things like Believing in Self and not just Being Satisfied as a By-Stander. I have several hundred more. (Send me your suggestions for **BS** pairs. As a "Thank you" I'll give you a 30% discount on that book!)

Right now, pick a subject, any subject. Begin your Subject Journal by answering these questions: Why did you pick this subject? What is so interesting about it? What would you do to improve it, or why would you leave it as it is?

Subject:[12]

_____

_____

_____

_____

_____

_____

_____

_____

_____

_____

[12] Stuck for a subject to use? Look in Appendix B.

Thought-For-The-Day (TFTD).

At some point every day, write down what you might call a "thought-for-the-day." (TFTD) It can be something someone has told you, something you read, a phrase you overheard, or a spontaneous thought occurring to you. If you generate a TFTD every day and record them diligently, you will find after a year you have your own inspirational book. Reading your TFTD from last year will inspire you for the generation of today's thought and the process becomes self-generating.

After a few years you will be able to go back to past journals of this type and reflect on your philosophy. If you do this everyday, both writing a new TFTD before or after reading and reflecting on last year's TFTD, the end result is that you have created a tremendous resource of information about you. Just as in any form of regular journaling, you are once again able to see seasonal patterns and overall life philosophies being revealed.

What is your thought-for-this-day?

_____

_____

_____

_____

_____

_____

_____

_____

(Please send me a copy of the TFTD you just wrote. Use the address on the copyright page or order form inside the back cover. You will be rewarded! — G.R.)

Special Event Journaling.

For significant events in your life, create a special journal. You may wish to have many people participate in recording their good thoughts in a special memory book of wishes, observations and remembrances for vacations, birthdays, anniversaries, weddings, holidays and even funerals.

On vacations and holidays, encourage everyone in the family to keep their own journal. After several months have passed, have a vacation memory party where everyone shares their memories.

My wife, Pam, and I treasure the journals written by our sons at ages 7 and 9 while on vacation. We also immensely enjoy reading the daily journals we both wrote while I baby-sat the boys at age 9 and 11 as my wife took a three-week tour of England as a tour guide for her aunt.

Community Journaling.

Created at birthday and anniversary celebrations, a community journal is much more permanent than greeting cards, and there is never a possibility of duplication. Community journals have several authors over multiple years. Use the same book year to year, building a history of the person or couple, their friends and family. This kind of journal can give hours of pleasurable memories, especially to the elderly as they reminisce about their lives.

A written journal is a marvelous gift for the bride and groom, graduates and award winners. Use multiple journals and pass them from guest to guest at the ceremony and reception. Such a gift will be treasured far longer than the gifts of linens, silverware, toasters, plaques and trophies.

Special event and community journals are wonderful gifts to parents and relatives, especially if prepared over a long period of time by several people. A quick way to create a memorable journal is to record the thoughts and greetings of all the people visiting during a family celebration. For example, every year at Thanksgiving time, our family reflects upon the events of the previous year by completing, in writing, sentences that start "This year I am thankful for . . ." with an entry for each letter of the alphabet. After dinner, instead of heading for the couch, we go around the table, one random letter at a time, saying our words and making comments. It becomes a very touching, humorous and enjoyable time. We keep these sheets of paper, and over the years it is interesting to see how our lives have changed.

Finally, (no pun intended) journals created at a funeral, written by the mourners in memorial to the deceased, will provide comfort and a clear expression of love to the survivors. After the immediate pain and the first few months of loss have passed, this kind of journal provides a source of remembrance and appreciation for generations to come. It becomes a memorial in the finest sense.

If Not for You, for Your Children.

Journaling provides the ability to record your perspective and philosophy of life for posterity. This means your children, your grandchildren, great-grandchildren, and later generations will have available to them the journals you have written, filled with the ideas and observations you had during your lifetime.

Certainly anyone would be delighted to have the diary or the journaling of a grandparent or a great-grandparent from many years ago. It would be an education (and probably an inspiration) to understand what they thought about in a different age. The same thing will be true for your descendants.

Your journals will become a treasure, filled with information for generations yet to come. Chances are these writings will be valued for two reasons. One, because of the relationship to you, their ancestor, and two, because not many people keep journals. Any form of a journal is quite rare.

My mother, Geraldine Edith (Ream) and father Edwin Adolf Reid, wrote to each other every day for over two years during World War II. My dad returned my mom's letters with his, and my mother kept them all. I have them now, and the collection is one of my most valuable possessions. I plan to glean my parents philosophy about life from the letters and publish them as a memorial to their lives and journaling effort.

If not for your children, for others.

Even if your journals are thrown away or sold at a garage sale, you never know, someday, someone may pick up *your* journal and begin reading. In reading your thoughts, they may become inspired to do more with their lives simply because you took the time to write your thinking down today. (Maybe an archeologist in 5148 A.D. will find your journal, the only known record to survive the global disaster mentioned in the introduction to this book.)

Your journaling is your unique history. It will reveal and describe the individual called "you." The person who will learn most from your journaling will be you. If other people learn something from your journals, that is a bonus. Journaling is the only way you will be able to accurately revisit, years later, what was important to you in earlier times in your life. Finally, the process of your journaling will inspire others to journal.

As you journal, you will most likely come across some lighthearted ideas and perspectives. To take full advantage of the lighter side of life . . .

5. Create a Humor File.

Nothing will give you more smiles over the years than the occasional browsing through a file of humorous clippings. This file is a place where you store the gems found in trade publications, newsletters, magazines and newspapers, plus those non-business inter-office jokes and memos showing up from time to time.

News Flash:

> ## Water pills cause major flooding near army base.
>
> An army truck carrying 15 tons of dehydrated water caused major flooding in Watertown county yesterday when it jack-knifed and fell into a small creek . . .

Keep a copy of inter-office cartoons, poems and essays. These are usually the 37th copy of a 37th copy, but the disintegrating image adds a bit of humor in and of itself. With the ever improving quality of copiers, even the lousy images themselves will bring back fond memories some day; "Remember when the latest joke or cartoon looked like someone had spilled coffee and cookies on it?"

Frequent flyer update:

> From an airline magazine article on risk:
>
> "While each year in the United States 50,000 die in automobile accidents, around 200 die in scheduled airline accidents. (In 1980 there was only one fatal scheduled airline accident.)"
>
> Hmmm...wonder what time that flight was scheduled to leave?

In the high-tech industries, many items funny today will have an extra humorous twist years from now. As technology changes, younger people will not understand the humor. Other items will get even funnier with age as we look back to the era of simpler (or maybe more complex) situations. Finally, some clippings will take on completely new perspectives, adding irony to the humor of the past.

> **Tid-"bits" from the late 1960's in the computer room:**
>
> **Notes attached to card decks:**
> "Please compile this program twice. I need two copies of the listing."
> "This deck was dropped. Be sure to read it in original order."
> "Some of this program is missing, but I'll figure that out after it is executed."
>
> **Comments found buried in program listings:**
> "John Smith says it is impossible for the program to reach this message."
> "If the next line ever gets executed we are in deep trouble."
> "The following lines of code are not necessary but are placed here just in case."
> "I still don't understand why the following line is needed."
> "If you are as uncertain as I am about this logic, the following line will really confuse you."

Items for a humor file include, but should never be limited to, cartoons, poetry, stories, articles and misprints. I have found a randomly organized humor file is just fine, but be sure to date each item. I have many times wished I knew both date and source of an entry so I could get legal permission to re-use it. You may want to use your clippings in preparing the company newsletter, an education program, special events, or even your own book, so keep good records.

Weird things I have heard said during business presentations:

"I'll just bullitize and go through the list."

"It can self-configure itself."

"This problem has to be solutioned, now!"

"It is a super-set of ease-of-use."

"This is a development thingy."

"I'm not rearview mirroring this, I'm crystal balling it."

Having some simple categorization will make this diverse little hobby even more interesting. Create files for humor dealing with people, politics, technology, systems, management, or whatever. It doesn't matter how you organize it so long as you capture it.

Performance Appraisal Time:
How to Interpret What the Boss Says
to You

Terms	Meaning
Active socially	Drinks heavily
Zealous Attitude	Opinionated
Forceful	Argumentive
A keen analyst	Thoroughly confused
Conscientious	Scared
Exceptionally good judgment	Lucky
Career minded	Back stabber
Aggressive	Obnoxious
Strong principles	Stubborn
Coming along fine	About to be fired
Shows great promise	Related to the president
Meticulous	Nit picker

It isn't necessary to save everything you come across. This hobby can overrun a file drawer very quickly. Set some basic criteria for keeping an item. You must at least smile at the original viewing, maybe even a chuckle should be necessary to qualify it for submission to your file. Once you have a few dozen items in your file, you will find an occasional review will bring a smile to your face and inspiration to an otherwise stressful day.

> **When in doubt, ponder.**
> **When in charge, delegate.**
> **When in trouble, mumble.**

An excellent use of your humor collection will be in the selection of just the right tidbit to give to a peer, subordinate or superior when you recognize they are having a difficult day. The kindness you show through the shared humor will be long remembered. Maybe their humor file will grow just a little from your expression of thoughtfulness.

Back on the job, a lighthearted approach works well to build a friendly rapport with others. Another way to build rapport is to . . .

6. Do Things with Urgency and Commitment.

Nothing gets another person on your side faster than approaching their project as if it were the most important thing you have to do. To help get your enthusiasm fired up, make a conscious effort to express yourself using a pace and tone of voice slightly faster and slightly higher pitched than your normal speaking rate and voice. Especially important at the beginning of interactions with other people, this slightly accelerated and more animated demeanor projects a feeling of excitement. Continuing to appear enthusiastic about working with them and on their project will put you in a position they will quickly come to respect.

Why does your enthusiasm generate respect? Well, how would you feel about the intelligence, motivation and attitude of someone who was excited about your project? Obviously, that person is pretty sharp to see things the way you see them! Not many people out there are as sharp as you are, right?

But, what can you do if you really are **not excited** about the project? You may not like this answer:

"Fake It 'Til You Make It!" FITYMI

Yes, I am suggesting you lie to yourself. Tell yourself "This is the best thing since sliced bread!", "I like working with this person!", "This project turns me on!" Our unconscious mind does not know the difference between imagination and reality. If you continue the effort to be excited about the project, you will be!

This technique is the "Opera, Broccoli, and Beer" approach. Sometimes a person just needs time and repeated tries to acquire a taste for something they will come to love. Just like OBB, once we find we like this new project we won't be able to get enough of it, and the result will be an unprecedented success due to our enthusiasm for it!

Three attitudes about work.

There are **three attitudes** you can have when faced with an assignment to do a particular project:

1. **Turned on**, in favor of doing the work. You are enthusiastic, motivated and ready to go!

2. **Neutral**, neither for or against. You are neither turned on or turned off and you can take it or leave it.

3. **Turned off**, opposed to doing the work. You are antagonistic, fault-finding, unmotivated, and ready to quit!

Three situations about work.

There are also **three situations** relative to your control of your involvement in the work:

A. **You are the decision maker** regarding who works on this project.

B. **You can influence the decision maker** as to who works on this project.

C. **You have no decision or influencing ability** regarding who works on the project.

Three outcomes of work.

Finally, there can be **three outcomes** of the work you do:

   X.   **Complete success,** excellence, quality, satisfaction, enjoyment of the process, great team spirit!

   Y.   **Mediocre results,** meets standards, works good enough, ho-hum spirit.

   Z.   **Total failure,** substandard, unhappiness, dissatisfaction, aggravation, blame, disgust, anger.

Expected results (X, Y, Z) from the interaction of attitudes (1, 2, 3) and involvement control variables (A, B, C) are illustrated in the table on the next page.

		Attitude		
		1 Turned on	**2** Neutral	**3** Turned off
Involvement	**A** Decision	X Complete Success	FITYMI = X Take self off = X	
	B Influence	X Complete Success	FITYMI = X Influence = X	
	C Neither Decision or Influence	X Complete Success	FITYMI= X or GOOTW else Y or Z	FITYMI= X or GOOTW or **FAIL!**

Conditions 1A, 1B and 1C:

You have what you want, so do it! Expect result X.

Conditions 2A and 3A:

FITYMI and expect result X, or take yourself off the project and give it to someone who has a 1 attitude.

Conditions 2B, 2C, 3B and 3C:

You always have three choices:

I.   FITYMI and expect result X,

or

II.   GOOTW,NCA (Get Out Of The Way, No Comments Allowed.) This means to get out of the way of those who have attitude 1. Further, don't comment about the result because **you** chose not to FITYMI.

or

III.   (The third choice depends on which of the remaining attitude and control conditions exist.)

Conditions 2B or 3B. Influence the decision maker to take you off the project.

Condition 2C. Be prepared for the consequences of a Y or Z result, because X results demand 1 attitudes.

Condition 3C. Be prepared for the consequences of Z results. You are going to fail because of your attitude.

There are four major conclusions to this study. They apply to all conditions of life, no matter if it is a change you are facing, work assignments, people, politics, projects, what TV channel to watch, what to have for dinner, where to go on vacation — anything! To be successful, apply this simple four-step attitude check:

1. If you like the situation, make the best of it!
Enough said. Enjoy!

2. If you don't like the situation and can change things, change them!
This includes your assignments and your attitude. Then, get the best result from your decision. After all, it was your decision!

3. If you don't like the situation and can influence someone to change things, then get on with influencing it!
Once again, this includes your assignments and your attitude. Then, get the best possible results from the decision. After all, you influenced it!

4. If you don't like the situation and you cannot influence it, then simply get on with it!
Either FITYMI or you will fail. Ultimately, it is **your decision** of what to do with **your attitude**. When your attitude is aligned with success, life takes on a new sense of urgency. You, and all

those around you, become energized to accelerate on the road to success.

Doing things with a sense of urgency and commitment can easily become a habit. The more often you pick up your pace and raise your enthusiasm level the more often your system will experience the rush of a positive attitude. Once your attitude is right, everything else follows, including success. Go take a break now. You deserve it. But do it quickly, Bit-O-Attitudes[13] tend to evaporate if not consumed while fresh!

To give yourself time to take a refreshing break . . .

[13] See Chapter 1, Give Others What You Demand in Them.

7. Delegate Whenever Possible.

I have asked many audiences to "raise your hand if your technical abilities are below average." Of course, no one raises their hand! Virtually no one will admit they are below average. Unfortunately, this perspective interferes with our ability to delegate to other people the challenges we face. This perspective also limits our potential by restricting the amount of time and energy we have for learning new things.

Since the vast majority of people feel they are above average, another conclusion is that there are very few others, if any, who can do the task at hand better than we can.

> **Not delegating will cause you to become below average.**

Artificially invented or real, our perspective of being above average causes us to lack confidence in the abilities of other people, especially those with whom we directly compete for advancement — our peers.

Without the needed confidence in others, we want to do it all ourselves. We repeatedly allocate our precious time to doing what we already know, over and over again. We insist on doing it all ourselves. In attempting to do it all, we unknowingly rob ourselves of the time and energy necessary to grow and expand our abilities. As a result, our lack of technical growth compounds itself, and we find ourselves in the very situation we earlier denied. We have become below average.

Meanwhile, others have less to do. They have the time to educate themselves and advance beyond our abilities. They take advantage of their extra time to seek and acquire new abilities and they leave us behind, still "doing our same old thing."

We, the very people who refused to delegate because they, not us, were below average, find ourselves choking on their dust as they accelerate past us on their way to new opportunities.

Expect others to do it differently.

Another reason we do not want to delegate is because others will probably do the task differently than we would. Since no two people have exactly the same experiences and perspectives, it is quite logical they are likely to approach a task in their own unique way.

When we finally give in and delegate a task, it is natural for someone else to do things differently than what we would have done. However, provided the outcome is what was specified, it doesn't matter how the task was accomplished so long as it was completed satisfactorily and within the defined parameters and standards.

Delegating: Three possible outcomes.

To be more successful, we must frequently take a leap of faith, trust the other person's abilities, and let them try to do what we know we could do. Taking this step and delegating a task can result in one of three outcomes.

The first outcome is one where you delegate a task to be done, and the person who you delegate it to does a better job than you could have! (Don't you just hate it when that happens?) In this case, the other person makes a tremendous gain, you find out who might be your primary back-up (or competition), and the system gets the task done well.

The second case is when the other person does a job equal to what you would have done. The task gets completed and gets done with results the same as if you did it. (There is another positive outcome here — it is in the time available to you. We will examine this in a moment.)

The third situation occurs when you delegate to someone who cannot do the task as well as you. They attempt to do it and they fail. You have to re-enter the situation and do the task to make it right. On the surface, this may appear to negatively reflect on your ability to select the proper person to do the task.

Upon closer examination, there are significant counter-balancing opportunities to turn this situation into a positive outcome. Your ability to recover from the situation points out, all the more clearly, your superior knowledge and capabilities regarding the task. The more important opportunity here is to help the less competent person. Mentoring them to become more competent, you become a hero for having helped someone else grow. Further, you now have someone to whom you can comfortably delegate this task next time.

> **By delegating to others, we reallocate time for ourselves and our growth.**

The reallocated time and unused energy gained through delegation gives us the opportunity to accomplish three things. One, we can use the time to explore more advanced challenges and determine what we need to learn to be able to undertake the challenges. Two, we now have the time to learn the *ASK* necessary to complete the new challenges. Three, we have relieved ourselves from some of the stress of the repetitive work known to quickly burn us out as technical specialists.

Delegation makes the world go 'round.

Another argument for delegation is to consider where you would be if others had not given you the opportunity to test your limits. Had you never been given the extra trust to do more, you may have never achieved your current level of technical competence. (Of course, if you were just waddling along right now, waiting for others to give you opportunities to grow, you probably wouldn't be reading this book either. Self-starters seek both the growth found in new challenges, and take time to stay ahead of the average through reading and self-improvement studies. :-)

There comes a point in everyone's life when they begin to realize how much other people have given them. Mentors, leaders and mature professionals have a strong desire to give back to the system in tribute to the people who helped them in the past. Delegation helps you pay back the debt you owe to those who gave you significant opportunities to grow. You pay them back by giving growth opportunities to others.

A delegation summary.

Once you have delegated a portion of your activities to someone else, you allow yourself to explore new ideas and concepts. The old quickly falls away as you learn new things never experienced before. Your attitude is refreshed, skills are built and your knowledge grows. Meanwhile, you begin your process of maturing and becoming a mentor as you help others along their paths to the discovery of their own personal and professional potential.

I.D.T.A.

Several years ago I heard a wonderful success story about delegation. It gave me great encouragement to grow and expand my horizons. At the time, I assumed I would get better and better as a Senior Instructor with IBM. I believed I would continue in being very satisfied with this wonderful job for many, many years. New people were joining my department. I was asked to delegate some of my presentations to other less experienced instructors. "What? Give away my perfected presentations? No one can do them as well as I do!" I was wrong. Twice. My presentations were not perfect, and they could be done better.

The people joining the staff were competent, energetic and able to do the job to the established standard. Each of them treated me with respect and admiration[14] as if I had some kind of magic when I did my presentations. (I had no magic, I was just "doing my thing.") After only a few times presenting, they were doing a much better job

---

[14] Thank you — Pat Davis, Les Fenter, Rose Lovell, Patti Summerville and Marty Washington.

---

than I had ever done. ("Two large pieces of humble pie, please.")

It was around that time, Beverly Sills, a beautifully talented opera performer, announced her retirement from the stage.[15] Being a casual opera fan and knowing only a few performers by voice and name, I was very disappointed, as she was one of my favorites.

Soon after her announcement, she was interviewed on National Public Radio. She was asked why she would go into the management side of the opera right at the peak of her success as a performer. She said it was time for her to move on to something else and referred to a charm bracelet she wears. The letters I, D, T, A hang from it. She said it was a reminder that as you achieve a level of expertise, and once you are really good at something, there is no sense hanging on to it, for it is time to do something else.

She went on to say there is little, if any, challenge or growth once you have mastered a particular skill or accomplished a specific goal. You might as well give the opportunity to someone else. Let them learn it, and experience it. Let yourself move on to bigger and better things, because if you do not give it up to someone else (in our case, if you do not delegate it), you limit your own growth and your own potential.

---

[15] This story used with permission of Beverly Sills.

The letters on Beverly Sills' charm bracelet stand for

"I Did That Already."

Now that you have finished this chapter, you can say "I did that already!" It is time for you to find things that you have yet to do. Finding new and unique things to do is the best way for you to . . .

8. Stand Out from the Crowd.

One of the key ways for you to enhance your personal and professional image is to do positive things to help you stand out from the crowd. Many people, some without even thumbing through it, decided *ASK for Success!* will not help them grow. You, however, decided to invest in yourself.

Acquiring and reading this book is evidence of your desire to stand out from the crowd. Without a doubt, you will grow from your investment of time and money by reading this book and trying the strategies suggested. But what of the other people who just drifted by? They are the crowd. They blend in with all the others. You have decided to set yourself apart from the crowd. Congratulations!

Let your imagination work for a few moments on the following list of things that stand out from the crowd:

- A daisy in a bouquet of roses.
- A red sports car in a fleet of yellow cabs.
- A soprano in a chorus of baritones.
- Laughter in the midst of tears.
- A toe stubbed on a chair leg.
- Flashing red and blue lights in your rearview mirror.

In these examples, it is difficult at a later time to remember the fullest rose, the newest taxi, the bearded baritone, the sadness of the tears, the toe not stubbed, or the make of the car that was in front of you.

We are much more likely to remember the things that stand apart from their background:
- the list at the top of this page.
- the symmetry of the daisy.
- the pitch of the soprano.
- the person who was laughing.
- the stubbed toe.
- the speed on the speedometer.

If we can make ourselves stand out, especially in a positive way, we will be more vividly remembered. If someone remembers us, it opens the possibility of their recognizing us and the abilities we bring.

Certainly there are times when it may be best to blend in. For example: when the IRS is looking for someone to audit, when going through a radar trap at 15 over the speed limit in the rush hour, when the company announces the next batch of layoffs.

Two important concepts for controlling the direction and development of your journey to success:

> ## The time to blend in is when you want to be overlooked.

> ## The time to stand out is when you want to be recognized.

Standing out from the crowd allows you maneuverability. Be an observer of "the crowd" and the threats against it. If the crowd takes off in a particular direction, you may have to move out of its way to avoid being swept away by it. If there is a threat, inform the crowd. Being the one to inform the group of danger keeps all eyes on you and gives you protection at the same time. When you stand out from the crowd you are more likely to be recognized.

Spaced repetition.

Every advertising agency will tell you that two, thirty-second commercials will generate product recognition far better than one, sixty-second commercial. Furthermore, three, twenty-second commercials are even better and six, ten-second commercials will do better than all the others! The same principle is true for you. The repetition of a your name, face, product or service over a period of time is by far the most powerful way to stand out from the crowd.

Recognition has very little to do with doing a competent and deserving job. The first definition of "recognition" in the Random House Dictionary is "the act of identifying something previously seen, heard, known, etc." It is not until the sixth definition that we find "the expression of achievement in the form of some token of appreciation."

Standing out from the crowd is the way to be "seen, heard, known, etc." Only then will other people start to figure out whether or not you deserve "some token of appreciation."

> **People who repeatedly make their presence known over time, get recognized.**

I am not suggesting you covertly attempt to make yourself appear better than others. It is easy to be of greater significance than others — simply find and point out those who are of less significance; those who contribute less than you do. Doing this does not add to the overall achievement of the group.

I do suggest you find simple ways to help others become aware of your presence and contribution, repeatedly. If the decision makers in your organization do not even know your name, how likely are they to support your advancement over those whom they do know?

Ifeveryoneisdoingityouwillnotstandout.

Before you start reading the list of ideas for standing out from the crowd, it is important to note that if other people are doing it, especially if many people are doing it, then it's probably not going to be effective for you. If only a few people are doing it, it may be something you want to adapt for a short period of time.

FindyourownwayforYOUtostandout.

Look for creative and innovative ideas from within yourself. Find things to make you unusual and out of the ordinary. Use discretion, however, for the last thing you want to be remembered for is being too "far out." For example:

Othersothersothers YOU othersothers

. . . might be a bit of overkill.

Let *your* imagination generate the perfect strategy for *you*. The idea *you* create will give you much more satisfaction than one that was borrowed.

Here are some ideas of things to do to promote yourself. (Promotion means "to contribute to the progress or growth of."[16]) Use them as the catalyst for stimulating spin-off ideas of your own.

Logos and calling cards.

Contribute to the ability of other people to recognize you by creating a logo or special symbol. This is something you design to represent yourself and all the things you do. It may be a special symbol, a special phrase or something equivalent to what a company would do to create a logo many people would recognize over a period of time.

---

[16] American Heritage Dictionary

Your logo can be as simple as your signature. Sign your work with this representation of you. Your mark will become known by others over time and the idea may even be adapted by them. That is a good measurement in its own way. It is an acknowledgement of other people recognizing your uniqueness.

Once you have created your logo, you can put it on your wall, on all of the documents you create, everywhere you can legitimately display it. People will start to realize the many places and times where you have made an impact on the business. With your logo, you can create your own calling card, your own special name tag for meetings and conferences; something making you a little bit different than other people.

Shirts, Jackets and Caps.

Make your own special T-shirt, jacket or cap proudly displaying your logo. Incorporate your name in your logo. Wear it in public. Many times it will create a reaction from other people because they have never seen your logo before, and it will open the door for the possibility of your starting a conversation with them. You never know what may result. As a consultant, you may end up with a new client. As a business person, you may end up with a new customer, just from the conversation resulting from your jacket. In any case, it will get the social conversation going and it makes you stand out from the crowd.

Personalize your office.

We all tend to personalize our offices. They look a specific way because they are a reflection of who we are and the way we do business. Consider going a step further. Display your personal logo on the door. Be the only office with a map of the world on the wall, a jar of candy on the desk, fresh flowers every Tuesday, background music, a floor lamp or a collection of cow bells hanging from the ceiling.

G'day Mate!

An associate of mine has a neat way of getting people to remember him at conferences. He wears his name tag upside down. (It is probably because he's a native Australian and may be confused as to which way is "up.") It certainly gets people's attention and it does make him stand out from the crowd. Some people may think it looks silly, but they cannot deny remembering good ol' "what's-his-name." His gimmick makes him different from everyone else at the meeting. People tend to remember his name because of that. (If you plan to use this gimmick, I sure hope he's not at the same meeting.)

Thank you notes.

Be the rare person who sends thank you notes.[17] Sending thank you notes makes you stand out because most people don't take enough time to thank people for their efforts. You may want to send an annual "thank you for doing business with me" to all your business associates. Tell them what you are particularly thankful for during the last year and thank them for being part of your success.

Do your job in unique, identifiable ways.

Standing out from the crowd also means in the way you do your job. When your work is done, is it a little bit more complete, more detailed, more specific, more well documented than other people? Have you been sure to give a little more than was expected?

Doing something different or something more than others do will help you stand out. Little things can make big differences in the way people remember you:

- Deliver your reports in a checkered covers.

- Have pictures in addition to words in your presentations.

---

[17] See Chapter 15, Give Praise to Others.

- Record your phone messages with lively rather than ordinary boring greetings.

- Provide people with a treat whenever they attend one of your meetings; something as simple as a candy mint, walk-in music or small mementos.

- Include a Thought For The Day in memos.

Who would you rather do business with? The ordinary, average person, or one who is "outstanding" and makes life just a bit more interesting?

A Parable.

There were two zebras. One blended in with the crowd. One stood out from the crowd.

There was safety in numbers and the zebra who blended in felt pretty well protected from random attacks from the lions. One day a stranger with a rifle fired a shot into the herd. The shot felled one zebra. The herd panicked. Some zebras were shouting, "Stop! Stop!" But it was too late. Moments later, all of the zebras, as animals occasionally do, blindly ran off a cliff to their death.

On another day, in another place, the zebra who stood out from the crowd observed both the location and direction of the grazing herd and the prowling lions. Over time there were a few stampedes and the lone zebra had to move quickly out of the way of the herd. The lions got caught up in the chase and didn't even notice the lone zebra. On another occasion the lone zebra noticed a stranger approaching with a metal stick. Being skilled at moving quickly, this zebra was a difficult target and was quickly ignored. The lone zebra called to the herd, "Follow me!" They did. They trampled the hunter.

Now that you stand out from the crowd, expect to be recognized and rewarded. When these nice things happen to you . . .

9. Enjoy Recognition.

Highly technical people enjoy what they do and have a level of enthusiasm difficult to restrain. When recognized for outstanding achievement or invention, I have observed a tendency of technologists to respond in one of two ways, they either want to tell everyone exactly how they did it, or they mumble something to the effect of "Oh, it was nothing." The first response contributes in a negative way by causing the giver or the observer of the recognition to be overloaded with technical information meaningless to them. The second response contributes negatively by appearing to be a reaction of low esteem or pride in the technical effort.

When you receive recognition for your skills, no matter if it is a large cash award or a simple "Way to go!" choose a middle ground, by neither exalting nor humbling the achievement. A simple, sincere "Thank You" and a warm smile will go a long way in improving the people image of technical professionals.

There is no need to go into all the detail of why the recognition was well-earned. The fact the recognition occurred is evidence enough.

Likewise, there is no need to make little of the achievement. You have done your job well and you deserve to hold your head high. You have done what others could not or would not do. Be proud! You deserve all you receive.

Most of us were taught as children to humble ourselves. It does not help one's image to be arrogant or to give excessive self-praise. Humility is good for keeping clear in our minds the perspectives of others. It is also advisable to be humble in the eyes of God.

Sometimes people feel it is necessary to give us praise. In these situations, who are we to argue with their brilliant observation of our worth? Accept the praise and let it be a boost to your motivation and pride. Avoid the desire for additional self-praise. It will only serve to cheapen the praise given by others since it would appear you think the praise given is not sufficient and needs further amplification.

After the recognition, add a note to you Achievement Journal.[18] Record your emotional reactions, the reactions of other people and a specific and detailed description of the nature of the recognition and what you did to receive it.

Later, on one of those days when you are thinking, "They just don't appreciate my abilities!", review your achievement journal. It will do wonders by reminding you that the rewards *are* there, sometimes they just take a while to materialize.

---

[18] See Chapter 4, Keep a Journal.

Give yourself some recognition, right now. Fill in the certificate on the next page. Sign it and present to yourself. I'm not joking — do it! You'll be surprised how much mental fun this can be.

Be it known,

on the _____ day of

_____,

in the year _____,

_____

was awarded this certificate of
recognition for

completing this certificate with skill,

presenting and accepting it with a
positive attitude,

and knowing it was the most important
part of an otherwise ordinary day.

Signed,_____

In addition, I would like to personally recognize you for completing this portion of *ASK for Success!*

Imagine the scene:

Every person you have ever met or admired is in the audience. Friends, family, co-workers, political leaders, your peers, the executives and board of directors of your company are present, even your first grade teacher. There is not a dry eye in the house as we hear the following words spoken about you . . .

"Your diligence in seeking new information for the betterment of your life is an example that will be followed by generations to come. Your efforts to improve the world, to serve other people through your devotion and dedication to your specialization and expertise, will be forever remembered by those who humbly seek your knowledge and follow in the path you have trod.

"You have given yourself permission and time to grow and the results are clearly visible — Your personal and professional image has become the model for us all! We, the members of the communities and organizations you serve, humbly thank you for your unselfish leadership and example."

To generate a reputation that deserves accolades such as these . . .

0A. Always Deliver More than You Promise.

What happened to chapter 10? Why is this chapter not listed in the table of contents? Because I thought it was a good way to illustrate the very principle presented in the chapter.

This is a chapter you did not expect. In a way, I have delivered more than I promised in the table of contents. The real chapter ten is the next chapter, so this chapter is a bonus and it demonstrates "recursiveness." (I love the concept of recursiveness! It gives my brain a really neat feeling every time I find or do something recursive.)

Recursiveness is sort of a "walk your talk" concept. For example, here are some things that are recursive:

- a lecture on how to give a lecture.
- a video tape on how to produce a video tape.
- a book on how to publish a book.
- a journal about journaling.
- a brown bag storing other brown bags.
- the sentence "This sentence no verb."
- a list of recursive examples.

Enough about recursiveness. (Is that recursive? ;-)

When you commit to giving more than you promise, there is no better way to understand its value than by simply doing it. As you provide a service to other people, let your actions speak louder than your words. When you successfully give more than you promise, it will not be necessary to point it out.

Always giving more than is expected is one of the surest ways to establish yourself as an individual who cares about the success of others. In turn, people will come to you when they want the better than average job done because they know you will serve "beyond the call of duty," will "go the extra mile" and will bring "added value." (Clearly, giving more than you promise must be an ancient principle since there are so many clichés for it.)

> **Giving more than you promise does not mean to promise less than you plan to give.**

Promise exactly what you intend to deliver. *Then* find ways to deliver more. (Not listing this chapter in the table of contents was contrived. However, the idea to write about "always giving more" sprang from a brainstorming session on the possibility of numbering chapters in this book in "hexadecimal," the numbering system used by computer people.[19])

When your objective is to make it worth someone's time to do business with you, time becomes more valuable to you. This is because you are putting more of your energy into each moment. The end result is one of greater satisfaction, both yours and your customer, of a job well done. Satisfaction is a pleasurable feeling. Humans tend to want to repeat pleasurable actions. Chances are you will get more opportunities to serve than others who provide only the minimum of service and the minimum pleasure.

If you build it they will come.
One of the most touching films I ever saw was "Field of Dreams." It is about a man who hears a whispering voice saying "If you build it, they will come." I believe the message in that film is one of building your *ASK* and knowing the reward for your effort will eventually come, in one form or another. The act of envisioning your dream begins the process of making your dream become reality. Giving more than you promise is one way to build both your dream of success, and your reputation as one who brings extra value and performance to every situation.

---

[19] See the end of this chapter for more information about the hexadecimal numbering system.

You may ask, "Why deliver more? In some cases, people will not appreciate, acknowledge or care that I gave more than I promised. So why should I do it?" Because — "If you build it, *they* will come." "They" are the good feelings you will have within yourself.

Immediate gratification.

Many people are concerned about getting the reward for their efforts right now. If they don't see an immediate reward, they don't think it's worth going the extra few steps, expending the extra energy, or putting forth the extra effort. I believe when we take those extra steps, over time, the rewards will come.

You will become recognized as an individual who is above average because, by definition, you are giving more than the average. Recognition may take a long time to come. It might not come in the form of paychecks, or promotions, or formal recognition. In some cases, the recognition never comes in the way it was expected.

A final protest.

People tell me "Gerry, there are certain businesses and organizations you just don't understand. In my situation I will **never** get any recognition for all my extra effort, so why should I do it?"

My answer is this, "What if someone else in your organization adopts the philosophy of always giving more? Who is your employer going to lay off when times get tight? The average contributor or the above average contributor? Also, consider this: Why do you stay in that environment? Why stay with a company that fails to recognize you over a long period of time? If you choose to stay in a limiting position, you will, by definition, be limited — except for the extras you choose to contribute without reward."

> **The limits you put on yourself are far more damaging to your potential than any limits put on you by others.**

In many cases, doing an extra good job is reward in itself. Chances are, if you continue to do the good job, the reward manifests itself inside you, in knowing you are doing the best possible job.

The final reward always comes. If you don't get the reward on earth, you'll get the reward in heaven. Good people do finish first.

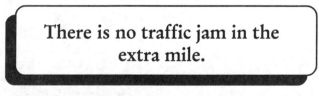

> **There is no traffic jam in the extra mile.**

— End of chapter —

And now for something completely different . . .

Even more than I promised, and maybe even more than you want, now follows. It is dedicated to all my high-tech computer friends. Without the computer industry I would still be delivering blueprints at General Motors (my first job) and I would never have had the good fortune to spend 30 wonderful years associated with the very people who inspired me to learn and grow.

After all those years you would think I could explain "hexadecimal" counting systems. So, as a thank you to all the master bit-twiddlers out there, I'm going to give it a try. If you are not into computer technology, you may want to by-pass the rest of this chapter. But if you skip to the next chapter, you'll never know the story of . . .

Why this is
Chapter 0A ("zero-alpha").

Being an old computer person (my computer is not old, I am) I thought it would be fun to surprise the reader, who in many cases is already a computer-type technical person, and call this chapter "Chapter A," which is what follows nine in hexadecimal. (Actually, the chapter should be, and is, "zero-alpha," which is more likely what an old computer person might call the value ten.)

One day, having temporarily decided to number the chapters in this book in hexadecimal, I challenged myself to come up with chapter titles starting with A, B, C, D E and F.

A — Always deliver more . . .

B — Believe in yourself . . .

C — Create a humor file . . .

D — Delegate . . .

E — Enjoy recognition . . .

F — Flatter others . . .

(Hmmm, creativity isn't so difficult after all!) Let's see, where was I? Oh, yeah . . .

"Bits, Bytes and Rock-and-Roll!"

In the world of computers, technical people sometimes use a numbering system quite different than the one most of us use.

Computers represent stored information in bits. A bit can be set on or off. A 1 indicates a bit is on and a 0 indicates a bit is off. For another reason (which I will not, because I cannot, explain), computers deal very well with sets of eight bits at a time. Eight bits are called a byte. (Do police computers take a byte out of crime?) However, people deal better with four bits at a time (a nibble?) and four bits have sixteen possible combinations of "on and off"-ness, from 0000 (zero) through 1111 (fifteen).

Now, on the surface, this is not a big deal until one is counting along "seven, eight, nine . . ." and this is where problems start. Most people count in a system called decimal (based on ten). When we go one past nine and arrive at ten, we simply "carry the one" to the left and start at zero again in the column where the nine was. Still with me?

Well, computer people have two problems they are faced with. First, since they only have 0 and 1 (the bit on or off) as soon as they get to two they have to "carry the one." Even though computer people say "zero, one, two, three, four . . ." the computer understands those numbers as

"0000, 0001, 0010, 0011, 0100 . . ." Here is the complete set of all sixteen combinations of four (0100) bits:

0	0000	zero
1	0001	one
2	0010	two
3	0011	three
4	0100	four
5	0101	five
6	0110	six
7	0111	seven
8	1000	eight
9	1001	nine
A	1010	ten
B	1011	eleven
C	1100	twelve
D	1101	thirteen
E	1110	fourteen
F	1111	fifteen

This system is called hexadecimal (hex (6), plus decimal (10), equals hexadecimal (16)).

The second (0010) problem is when computer people get to "nine" (1001). With four bits, there are still some combinations available to the computer (specifically, 1010, 1011, 1100, 1101, 1110 and 1111). If the people kept going with decimal counting, all of a sudden they would need two digits to express one set of four bits (specifically, 10 for 1010, 11 for 1011, 12 for 1100, 13 for 1101, 14 for 1110 and 15 for 1111). To keep things simple (who are they kidding?) instead of saying "nine, ten, eleven, twelve, thirteen, fourteen, fifteen," they say "nine, A, B, C, D, E, F." I'm not kidding! Seriously, they do this! But it kinda' makes sense because with one digit (zero though F) they can say any combination of 4 bits.

When they need to go past "F," which is fifteen, they carry the one to the left and start back at zero in the column where the F was! So now they can write "10" say "one-zero" and mean 16! (If you have come this far with me, hang in there, there's just a "bit" more to tell you.)

Now remember, the computer actually uses eight bits. So, if the people keep counting this way, with each number or letter they say representing one set of four bits, they can easily describe what is in any particular byte (eight bits) of the computer's memory.

		Eight bits (byte)		
Decimal	Number	4-bits	4-bits	What is said
1	one	0000	0001	"zero-one"
2	two	0000	0010	"zero-two"
3	three	0000	0011	"zero-three"
9	nine	0000	1001	"zero-nine"
10	ten	0000	1010	"zero-A" or "zero-Able"
11	eleven	0000	1011	"zero-B" or "zero-Baker"
12	twelve	0000	1100	"zero-C" or "zero-Charlie"
13	thirteen	0000	1101	"zero-D" or "zero-Dog"
14	fourteen	0000	1110	"zero-E" or "zero-Easy
15	fifteen	0000	1111	"zero-F" or "zero-Fox"
16	sixteen	0001	0000	"one-zero"
17	seventeen	0001	0001	"one-one"
18	eighteen	0001	0010	"one-two"

This chart would be very long indeed, if it were to illustrate all of the combinations up to 1111 1111 (fox-fox), because when all eight bits are turned on, the decimal value would be 255! In the long run, computer people are much better off with this kind of counting system because saying things like "two-C" or "dog-fox" to another computer person means the other person can understand which bits are set on or off for eight bits, or an entire byte, and wow, does this kind of talk ever turn them on!

Just for fun, try to figure out what "baker-six" (1011 0110) represents."[20]

If you are still confused and want to know more, go ask someone in the computer department to explain it. (By the way, this concept of "Give the problem to someone else," or "Pass the buck," or "Pass the byte" is **not** one of the attitude principles for success!)

While you are talking with computer people, be extra careful not to call them a "four-easy, six-five, seven-two, six-four, two-one." Such insults could really make them angry! They'll love it if you call them "forty-seven, seventy-five, seventy-two, seventy-five, twenty-one" but don't do it too often or it will give them a big head!

Before you go to the computer experts for help, it is a good idea to . . .

---

[20] Come on, no fair! Give it a try! If you insist, the decimal answer is 104+(((3x10)+9)x8)/4. (You didn't think I was just going to tell you, did you?)

---

10. Have a Ten-Second Commercial.

If you had just 10 seconds to tell someone about yourself, what would you say? Would they be impressed or bored? Would their curiosity be piqued? Would they remember you and what you have to offer?

Take ten seconds, right now, and say out loud your spontaneous response to "Who are you?" GO!

10, 9, 8, 7, 6, 5, 4, 3, 2, 1, 0!

(Obviously, it would help to have a friend act as a time keeper.)

What did you say (or think :-)? People respond in many ways to this exercise. References are made to name, history, family, heritage, job, calling, religion, education, title, accomplishment, etc. Rarely is the question spontaneously answered with any future reference. Most of the time the answer is whatever pops into their mind.

Ten-second commercials.

What if you were given a ten second commercial during the Superbowl? (No, you cannot have the cash equivalent :-) Imagine what such an exposure could do for your career, your dreams, your mission in life! Even if it were just a plug for your employer, you sure would want to have that ten seconds thought out. Isn't it the same situation, just with a smaller audience, when you introduce yourself to someone at a business or social interaction? You never know who you will meet. They may have a level of influence or a network of contacts to give you exactly the break you need for success. A well prepared commercial can make a world and a lifetime of difference.

To give you some ideas of what to say in your ten seconds, jot some notes with your initial reaction to these questions (a values journal):

What is important to you?

_____

_____

_____

_____

_____

_____

Why are you above average?

_____

_____

_____

_____

Why do you have value in your particular area
of expertise?

_____

_____

_____

_____

What do you stand for?

_____

_____

_____

_____

What would you die for?

_____

_____

_____

_____

_____

What do you live for?

_____

_____

_____

_____

_____

_____

_____

_____

_____

What do you hope is said in your eulogy?

_____

_____

_____

_____

_____

_____

_____

_____

_____

_____

What do you want inscribed on your headstone?

_____

_____

_____

_____

_____

_____

_____

_____

Now, given all the ideas you have recorded (journaled), write out exactly what you want to remember to say in a ten second response to:

"Who are you?"

_____

_____

_____

_____

_____

_____

_____

_____

_____

That is quite a challenge, isn't it? With this commercial in hand — practice, practice, practice. This is one time in your life you want to have something fully memorized. You can be spontaneous later as people ask you to tell them more about yourself. At this stage, concentrate on getting your introduction down and getting your delivery crisp.

And now a word from our sponsor.

"Hi, I'm Gerry Reid. I am a professional speaker, educator and author. I specialize in motivating people, encouraging their professional growth and helping them fully develop their personal potential."

Longer commercials.

The next levels of your self-introduction also need careful preparation and rehearsal. Separate from this book, in one of your new journals, create 30, 60 and 120 second introductions.

These longer introductions allow you to talk about many of the things you have noted in this chapter. Longer introductions do not need to be memorized. Matter of fact, to do so would be dangerous because if you forget where you are you would appear pretty silly not remembering who you are! You need to be able to repeat the major points in a confident and professional presentation.

There are many opportunities to practice. Give the 30 second version to a salesperson before talking about a major purchase. Give the one-minute version at the beginning of your next business presentation. Give the two minute version in response to someone saying, "tell me more!" (which is very likely to happen if your 10 and 30 second versions are good ones).

You never know when you will have the opportunity of a lifetime. Be prepared. If you have a chance to meet your CEO, a political figure, or any other person you want to influence, the first 10-30 seconds are critical. When interviewing a person you are considering for a position in your organization, your competent introduction will let them know the quality you are expecting in them.

To enhance your personal and professional image, stand out from the others with your introduction. Use your introductions as often as possible: in social situations, when greeting strangers who happen to sit next to you on an airplane, when meeting others on civic, community or other committees. The more you hear your own introduction the more it will build your confidence and give you pride in who you are.

It's one thing to have a commercial prepared and ready to go. What is even more important, is to expand your introduction and be able to . . .

11. Describe Your Abilities Clearly.

Technical people interact and communicate with basically two types of people: those who understand the language of technology and those who don't. A technical peer has little difficulty understanding the content of your communication, written or verbal. While the *ASK* of interpersonal communication between people are always important, technical peers are usually most concerned with the information contained in the message. A non-technical person, on the other hand, may not fully understand the content of the communication. They place much greater value and demand on the interpersonal communication ability of the technologist.

A highly successful technologist can communicate well with both technical and non-technical people about both their technical and non-technical abilities. To help develop these two skills, practice being able to do the following four exercises:

1. Given 30 seconds, describe to a **highly technical** person your most powerful **human attribute.**

2. Given 30 seconds, describe to a **highly non-technical** person your most powerful **technical ability.**

3. Given 30 seconds, describe to a **highly technical** person, your most powerful **technical ability.**

4. Given 30 seconds, describe to a **highly non-technical** person your most powerful **human attribute.**

These four distinctly different exercises are extremely challenging, especially considering they may all be needed in the space of just a few minutes during a meeting or discussion with you or about your technical ability.

When talking with people who are not experts in your area of expertise, explain things in the terms a 16 year old would understand. Explain things in terms your spouse, mother, or father would understand. Explain things in terms the CEO would understand. Focus your attention on **their reactions**, not on how much you know.

Watch for even the most subtle signs of misunderstanding. A furled brow, squinted eye, or tilted head may signal a miscommunication is developing. Such body language can indicate a conflict on content (the technical message) or with attitude, tone or personality. One must deal with these conflicts differently with technical and non-technical people, and differently depending on whether the conflict itself is technical or non-technical.

Communication with a technical person about a technical subject seems to be an easy assignment. Both people understand the jargon of the job, or do they? Today's technical languages are constantly evolving as new methodologies, products, services and applications evolve. If there is conflict or confusion regarding content and you are dealing with a technical person, it may be a good idea to go deeper into defining the technical concept and its relationship to other technical matters.

If the conflict or confusion is with a person who does not understand the technology, it is probably best to back away from a deeper definition and ask questions to see what level of information is understood. Non-technical people want to avoid being talked down to. They do not want to be made to appear ignorant or uninformed. They want to understand things in terms of the end result of the technology, not the process of the system or procedure used to get them there.

When there is conflict outside the technical message, many times it does not matter whether the other person is technically or non-technically oriented. Dealing with personal conflict requires practice in asking non-threatening questions to get to the cause of the difference. What a person knows or is able to do is not the problem in this situation; therefore, this kind of communication deals with attitude.

One very simple technique to use is to find out if the other person is understanding you by asking:

> ## "Am I presenting this information in an understandable way?"

If the answer is "Yes" — This is an ideal time to have the other person restate in their own words their understanding of what you are presenting. This allows you to verify the correctness of their perception.

If the answer is "No" — It is pointless to continue the presentation since it would only be building more confusion upon the existing confusion. This is the ideal time to have the other person express what they **do** understand. You can then build upon what they **do** know.

Both of these situations point out the need of presenting new information starting where the recipient is. In education it is called "going from the known to the unknown." Too often technical people begin with what they know and try to work backwards to the listeners position. It is far more productive to start with the simple, then present, step by step, how to get to the complex. Along the way, check for understanding frequently.

Once your introduction is clear and concise, you can begin to move on to the task at hand, which is to . . .

12. Sell Your Ideas Well.

ISTAR is a simple mnemonic to help you remember a very powerful pattern of selling your ideas and services.

> "I bring you new Ideas. These ideas take the form of new Systems. These new systems produce new ways of Thinking about the business. It is in this new thinking that new Applications can be designed. The new application will bring you new Results."

Ideas,

    Systems,

        Thinking,

            Applications,

                Results

ISTAR

- Analyze Ideas
- Understand Systems
- New Thinking
- Better Applications
- Improved Results

Whenever we are presented new information, there is a change in the pattern of our thinking. The new pattern initiates new actions thus improving upon the results we were previously getting. Communicating this simple sequence is an excellent way to sell your ideas successfully.

When approaching a client or customer, think in terms of their perspective. They have patterns of thinking producing results now. You need to be able to convince them that your new pattern of thinking will produce results of greater value to the client than what they are currently getting. These new patterns of thinking may be called applications, systems, procedures or any number of other technical terms. The bottom line is: there needs to be a change for the better in at least one of four elements of work: Resources, Effort, Time, Results.

Resources: These are the **things purchased** to produce products or services.

- Materials to build a product.
- Machinery to shape and assemble the materials.
- Research and Development.
- Facilities.
- Maintenance of the above.
- The salaries and benefits of the people operating the machinery and executing the processes.
- Education, training, motivation and maintenance of the people.

Effort: This is the **energy needed** to produce the product or service:

- Electricity.
- Heat.
- Strength or capacity (of people and machinery).
- Endurance (of people and machinery).

Time: The only element of this model supplied at a constant rate in the work process. We cannot create additional time. We can only reallocate the constant amount we have. Time can be expressed in terms of:

- Duration of a given process.
- Speed at which people or products move through processes.
- Amount (of time) consumed in acquiring resources.
- How long a specific amount of energy will power the process.

Results: While not a part of the **process of work,** results can be looked at as a measurable variable when comparing the effect of changes in other elements. A change in results may be observed in several ways:

- Quality
- Competitiveness
- Market Share
- Features
- Performance
- Demand

Successful selling using the elements of work.

The user of our product or service may question why things must change. The answer for them is in the productivity of the result of the change. They want to know things like: "Will I . . .

- get more results in the same time?"
- get more results with the same effort?"
- get more results using the same resource?"
- get the same results in less time?"
- get the same results with less effort?"
- get the same results with less resources?"
- need less resources"?
- need less time?"
- need less effort?"

In response to this growing list we sometimes want to shout "OK! OK! Enough! Stop!"

These questions point to the need to clearly understanding the impact of change on the four work elements previously mentioned: Resource, Time, Effort, Results. Examining the next two tables, we begin to see the way the user of our technical skills measures the worth of our service. We must respond accordingly, in terms the user demands.

The following table illustrates the premise that it is "Good" to change a single work element for the better as long as no other work element is affected. Any one of the intersections marked "Good" is likely to please the user of our services.

Table D.

Reaction to changing a single element of work.

		Change in a single work element:			
		Less Resource	Less Effort	Less Time	More Results
Same amount of:	Resource		Good	Good	Good
	Effort	Good		Good	Good
	Time	Good	Good		Good
	Results	Good	Good	Good	

What is even more desirable is a combination of changes building on a simple "Good" and making it into something better. This combination is illustrated in the next table.

Table E.
Reaction to changing multiple work elements.

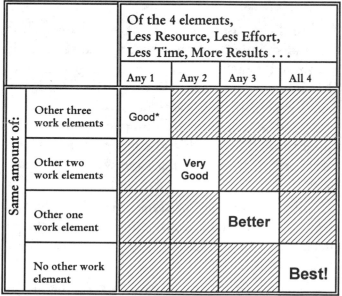

		Of the 4 elements, Less Resource, Less Effort, Less Time, More Results . . .			
		Any 1	Any 2	Any 3	All 4
Same amount of:	Other three work elements	Good*			
	Other two work elements		Very Good		
	Other one work element			**Better**	
	No other work element				**Best!**

*This intersection represents the entire content of Table D.

Clearly, if we can produce a positive effect on multiple elements of the work process, the user of our products and services is likely to grow more and more satisfied with the changes being proposed.

To help sell your ideas to others, build a case similar to these two tables. The simpler the better.

1. Show the impact of one change and the corresponding benefit.

2. Acknowledge the feelings of discomfort while going through the change.[21]

3. Emphasize that the benefits will far outweigh the uncomfortable feelings associated with the change.

To build the case in support of the change, show the added impact of the second change and the multiplied benefits as the two changes interact. Continue, step-by-step, adding the third and fourth elements. (Please note, this model is presented as a base of thinking for your creative application. The words and concepts you put into your presentation are not the words presented here.)

The following patterns are intended to stimulate your conceptual thinking of what is meant by "Very Good," "Better" and "Best" intersections in the last chart.

Begin by thinking of the direct, one-on-one benefits being offered:

1 change = 1 benefit.

2 changes = 2 benefits.

3 changes = 3 benefits.

4 changes = 4 benefits.

---

[21] See Chapter 19, Embrace Change, for further strategies for dealing with the resistance to change.

Next, move on to explain how the changes interact with each other in a cumulative way. Let's examine a project with four elements to be changed: A, B, C and D:

1 change (A only) = 3 benefits, one each as

A improves B, C and D.

2 changes (A and B) = 6 benefits:

1, 2, 3 as A improves B, C, D.

4, 5, 6 as B improves A, C, D.

3 changes (A, B, C) = 9 benefits:

1, 2, 3 as A improves B, C, D.

4, 5, 6 as B improves A, C, D

7, 8, 9 as C improves A, B, D

4 changes (A, B, C, D) = 12 benefits:

1, 2, 3 as A improves B, C, D.

4, 5, 6 as B improves A, C, D.

7, 8, 9 as C improves A, B, D.

10, 11, 12 as D improves A, B, C.

Third, begin to explain the synergistic effect of each change by **multiplying** the effect of each on the other:

1 change = 1 benefit

2 changes = 2x2 = 4 times the benefit.

3 changes = 3x3 = 9 times the benefit.

4 changes = 4x4 = 16 times the benefit.

The fourth and final presentation can build on the multiplication of the entire set. For every effect of A impact there is the effect of B *and* the effect of C *and* the effect of D. Think in terms of factorial multiplication of four components:

A x B x C x D

4 factors,

4 factorial,

4! = 4 x 3 x 2 x 1 = 24 times the benefit!

This strategy of building a case for the benefit of change can also be used to explain the complexity of multiple simultaneous change and the corresponding risk. Using the same process, and building the case **against** change, will help people understand the growing risks associated with multiple changes occurring at the same time.

In either case, you are selling your ideas well by examining, in a step-by-step progression, the features, benefits and effects of the proposed change.

Whenever you find yourself in a situation requiring selling or information gathering . . .

13. Ask Questions.

Questioning, the act of asking someone to reveal information, is one of the most powerful communication skills available, and it is one of the easiest to obtain. With dedicated practice, the skill of powerful questioning can be mastered quickly. The ability to question properly is one of the most rewarding ways to establish a reputation of being a caring and friendly person. Unfortunately, questioning is one of the most overlooked and misused skills of today's professional.

Try this on for size: If I were to ask you to tell me "How did you come to be in the profession you are in?" To answer, you would have to make several statements, maybe even several paragraphs to satisfactorily explain how you got to the position you now hold. On the other hand, if I had asked "What do you do for a living?" You probably would have taken just a few statements, to describe your job.

One powerful way to get others to open up their communication to you (and the information that goes along for the ride) is to ask "How?" questions. Put these questions in a form that requires answers that describe events over time.

The person you are communicating with is probably willing to give some information, just for the sake of politeness, but the really valuable information is given when they feel there is something in it for them. They are tuned into the world's most powerful radio station:

WIII-FM
"What Is In It — For Me?"

Powerful questions help in gathering information for the questioner. These questions also help the person being questioned to gather the experiences and thoughts to successfully answer the questions with quality and accuracy.

Whenever you ask a question, be certain it is helping the person being questioned as well as yourself. The question you ask should help them make a decision, put together a history, identify what is important to them, or clarify what they want.

"Will you help me . . ."

One particularly useful technique to use is to preface any question with a form of "Will you help me . . . ?" This format makes the person being questioned aware that they are doing someone else a favor or service. Most people feel good about helping someone else.

"Will you help me . . ." is especially helpful in establishing new relationships with people who have the information you need, but have yet to work with you for any period of time. It gives them the chance to feel useful and supportive and to leave a good impression with you, because they are helping you answer the questions.

Older, more established relationships can be refreshed in a positive way as other people begin to realize you have become more aware of their value. Their value is in both the information they have and in their ability to help you learn what they know. In all cases, the working together (helping each other) can quickly form a team spirit — a sense of partnership. Don't forget, however, to keep in mind the original thought of WIII-FM. Your partner in the discovery or revelation of new information must always feel there is personal gain for them in helping you attain your goals.

If you were to adopt the psychological approach of making your client feel good about themselves, they will want to help you above all others, because they enjoy receiving your appreciation and respect. They will go out of their way to help you because they know it will make them feel good about themselves.

Expect to be turned down or misunderstood occasionally when asking for information. It takes time to practice and develop questioning skills. The goal of practice is to hone your skill so your needs and intentions become clear to the other person.

By establishing the WIII-FM and "Will you help me" patterns, the people on the receiving end of your questions will go out of their way to help you get through any problem of misunderstanding. They may even offer to explain why they must turn you down on some requests, such as why some information is confidential, or proprietary. Certainly, after having built a strong relationship through excellent questioning, the last thing they want is to be caught in the trap of having to say, "Now that I've told you top secret information, I'll have to kill you. Sorry."

When you don't have the answers, admit it.

Never hesitate to admit you do not have all the answers. Taking a humble or subordinate posture may help you get even more information. In doing so, you open the door even wider for the other person to feel a sense of helping you learn what you need.

Admitting you do not have all the answers will also help you learn in what situations others have the edge on you. Even though this may seem like a negative perspective, it may be necessary in establishing a long-term relationship. Once others know you are not trying to outdo them, they will again become an asset to you by giving you the information you need. You will no longer be a threat to them. The two of you may well be on the road to establishing a strong partnership.

During the establishment of this new partnership about information, if the information exchange has less quality than you expected, turn the situation to a future focus. Look at the current situation as just a small bump on the way to a long-term partnership with great rewards to both parties.

The major message here is to be aware of the use of good questioning skills in the making of a friend and ally in the person you are questioning.

Question asking strategies.

The quality and clarity of any information exchange can be improved with the use of proper questioning techniques. First, there are three questions for general use. Due to their tremendous power, these questions must be used with care, diplomacy and respect to avoid causing friction, irritation and aggravation.

1. **Listen for nouns and verbs** having more than one meaning. Take the noun or verb in question and substitute it in the following question:

- "When you said '(repeat the noun or verb),' what did you mean, specifically?"

Examples:

> "When you said 'pretty soon,' what
> did you mean, specifically?"
> "When you said 'the project', which
> project were you referring to?"

2. Listen for implications that there are restrictions, limits or extremes. These are words or phrases such as "should/should not, can/cannot, must/must not, ought/ought not, everyone, nobody, never, always." Substitute the restriction, limit or extreme in this question:

- **"What will the result be if we (imply the restriction, limit or extreme is ignored)?"**

> or, simply repeat the word
> as a question:

- **"(restriction, limit, extreme)?"**

Examples:
"The meeting is mandatory."

> "What would the result be if I don't
> attend the mandatory meeting?"

"Everyone must file an income tax return."

> "Everyone?"

---

3. Listen for direct or indirect comparisons. Clarification of what is being compared will significantly increase the chances of understanding the implication and meaning of the comparisons.

If the comparison is direct ask:

- **"In what way is "(substitute the direct comparison)?"**

Example:
"That process is better."
    "Better than what?"

If the comparison is implied ask:

- **"Compared to what?"**

Example:
"This is an important project."
    "Compared to what other projects?"
"Productivity is down."
    When you say "productivity" what do you mean, specifically?
    "In what way is productivity down?"
    "Productivity is down? Compared to what?"

More Examples:

"Operations cannot continue this way!"
> "What will the result be if we continue this way?"
>
> "Which operations are you referring to, specifically?"
>
> "What way?"

"All of those people do not care anymore."
> "Who do you mean when you say 'those people ?'"
>
> "When you say they don't care, what do you mean, specifically?"
>
> "All of them?"

These examples may seem silly taken out of the context of normal conversations. The principle remains. The quality of communication with other people is dependent on clear understanding of information exchanged.

Notice also, how the awareness of these questions affects the way you might give information. Realizing how unclear day-to-day conversations are will help you communicate better. Knowing about unclear nouns, verbs, restrictions, limits, extremes and the use of comparisons will significantly improve your ability to present information to others.

Applying any of these questions frivolously will quickly destroy the rapport between people. Use them when there is legitimate confusion about the communication. When used properly, these questions help both the person asking and the person answering. In other words, be certain the question will help clarify information for all parties concerned.

A good rule of thumb is: If you have a question in mind, ask it. Chances are very good other people have the same question in their minds, but are not assertive enough to ask it.

There are several additional questions that invite the receiver to open up and supply the information you need to do a better job or to understand the needs of the person you are with. Useful in any situation, the following five questions are especially powerful in marketing and negotiating situations.

1. "How did you come to . . .
    be in this business?"
    that conclusion?"

    _____?"
    (create your own)

2. "What is it you most enjoy about . . .

     your business?"

     the possibilities of this agreement?"

     _____?"

     (create your own)

3. "What advice would you give a less
    experienced person about . . .

     your business?"

     dealing with these issues?"

     _____?"

     (create your own)

4. "What one thing would you do if . . .

     you had unlimited resources?"

     you knew we could not fail?"

     _____?"

     (create your own)

5. "What would make you the . . .

     most satisfied with your business?"

     proudest of our accomplishments?"

     _____?"

     (create your own)

Here are five bonus questions and statements guaranteed to open up the flood gates of information:

6. "Please explain."

7. "Why is that?"

8. "What does that mean to you?"

9. "What is it you want?"

10. "How can I help?"

The people you communicate with are interested in their success. If you present yourself to them as one who is sincerely interested in their success, they will go out of their way to do business with you.

With proper questioning it will be easy to . . .

14. Communicate in Parallel with People.

Imagine these two scenarios:

Scenario 1.

Chris: "Man, the workload is terrible! I'm so overloaded with things to do I can't even find time to breathe!"

Pat: "Yeah, it's the pits! I'm always asked to do more than is physically possible — and with no appreciation when I do it!"

Chris: "Geeze, you said it. I'm never appreciated for all my extra effort, and everyone else gets pats on the back for doing less than I do!"

Pat: "That's the truth! No one does more around here than you and I do, and what do we get for it? Nothing!"

Chris: "Even less! Just yesterday I went out of my way to do something extra and Lynn never even acknowledged it!"

Pat: "I know what you mean — especially Lynn. I can never do enough to make that turkey happy."

Scenario 2.

Chris: "Let me tell you, I think the whole thing is immature. They should put someone with experience in charge!"

Pat: "You bet! Together we could show them a thing or two."

Chris: "Heck yes! If they only had any idea of what we know, they'd tremble in their boots."

Pat: "All I know is I'd like to have just one day in charge. I'd show them how to do it right!"

Chris: "I'm with you! Those jerks need a eye opening experience!"

Pat: "They'll learn someday who's the boss. For now, I'm just going to watch them suffer."

Is there anything good about these two conversations? In both cases the pair are communicating in parallel. Both headed, marching in unison, either down to the pits of "poor me" or up to the heights of "holier than thou."

Communication in parallel is extremely powerful in building personal and professional camaraderie. But be careful! The examples given show that when we are in sync, there is a feeling of power within the conversation. A power that can take us both to where neither of us wants to be. Is there any hope for these situations? Yes, of course.

Parallel communication means to get in step with your communication partner in a way that assures you both are walking the same path. Over time, take the initiative and gently lead your partner to the middle ground of parallel, adult communication. There, you will find neither a sniffling child, nor a domineering parent. Strive for the productive ground of adult-to-adult conversation. Be aware, the power of parallel communication will quickly draw the unsuspecting to a non-productive, but very enjoyable journey if both people are not careful.

Remember also, the power of questioning. Carefully chosen questions, especially closed ended ones, can help redirect a conversation headed for trouble.

In scenario 3, a variation of scenario 1, Pat parallels the tone for just a moment and then takes Chris to a more adult tone:

Scenario 3.

Chris: "Man, the workload is terrible! I'm so overloaded with things to do I can't even find time to breathe!"

Pat: "Yeah, it seems to be a busy time. Are you working on Project X?'

Chris: "Yes, and Projects A through W! I'm never appreciated for all my extra effort, and everyone else gets pats on the back for doing less than I do!"

Pat: "Well, sometimes everyone is loaded down. Do you think a team meeting would help?"

Chris: "Maybe, but that will just take extra time for the meeting!"

Pat: "How about a brown bag lunch meeting? That should not have too much of an impact on everyone's time."

Chris: "Well, OK, let's give it a try, but YOU tell Lynn!"

Pat: "No problem, consider it done."

Scenario 4, is a variation of scenario 2. The strategy of being more adult in the conversation is applied after Chris recognizes a bad pattern has formed:

Scenario 4.

Chris: "Let me tell you, I think the whole thing is immature. They should put someone with experience in charge!"

Pat: "You bet! Together we could show them a thing or two."

Chris: "Heck yes! If they only had any idea of what we know, they'd tremble in their boots."

Pat: "All I know is I'd like to have just one day in charge. I'd show them how to do it right!"

Chris: "Well, that's not likely to happen. Do you think maybe we have a communication problem with them?"

Pat: "I don't know, I guess so. But how are they going to learn who's boss?"

Chris: "What if we started an informal newsletter, sort of like a press release each week. Would that help?"

Pat: "Sure, but I'd rather see them suffer a little."

Chris: "Tell you what, let's be advocates for positive communication rather than adversaries. OK?"

Pat: "OK. Where do we start?"

In all these illustrations, the leader of the conversation is the professional who knows that paralleling another will establish rapport. Once

---

the rapport is in place they can lead the "not so professional" person to a more adult level. This also avoids the conflict of arguing and the equally unhelpful extremes of demanding parents or whining children.

No matter what mode of communication you find yourself in, be certain to frequently . . .

15. Give Praise to Others.

Do you enjoy getting a nice "Thank you!" from time to time? It brings a smile to the face and a feeling of pride and satisfaction to the heart. Once acknowledged in this way, have you ever noticed a tendency to want to do more for the person who gave the praise? Most people do, especially when there is no doubt the praise is sincere and deserved.

> **Giving praise to others will quickly accelerate the support others give you.**

Seek opportunities to praise and flatter others. Thanking others for simply being there and being part of the team will instill in them a positive image of you. It will become more evident you are aware of their contribution and appreciate their efforts.

When people do more than is expected, there is a special need to make notice of their contribution. However, a person does not have to do something extraordinary before praise is given.

Acknowledge others even at times when they are simply doing their normal job. It will signal them that you are changing and becoming a more appreciative observer.

The process of finding things to acknowledge is an excellent exercise in fine-tuning your observation and awareness skills. You become more sensitive to the individual's perspective when you are focused on them rather than yourself. This new sensitivity will quickly be noticed by others and you may find compliments and acknowledgements about you increase rapidly. This is not the objective of giving praise to others. It is, however, one of the profitable by-products.

Practice looking for things deserving special comment. In doing so, you will become more aware of what others **do** contribute. This higher level of awareness opens your mind and perception to more of the events surrounding you. As you grow in awareness, you are better able to see, hear and feel the benefits of further growth. It is a self-perpetuating situation — the more you grow, the more you **can** grow and the more you will **want** to grow.

As your mental acuity of the events surrounding you increases, so will your sensitivity to the thoughts running through your mind. You will hear yourself thinking positive thoughts about people more frequently. The key is to take advantage of those thoughts and take action. Whenever you are struck with a thought suggesting you should take action to praise, thank or endorse someone, do it without fail. Make it a habit.

Follow through.

Have you ever found yourself thinking about doing something special in response to the current situation? Even when this thought is full of emotion and positive images of the result, what usually happens? Nothing! The enthusiasm of the moment quickly fades away and we fail to follow through with our good intentions.

Let me propose an imaginary situation. Let's suppose (just for the sake of illustration) there have been two points in your reading of this book where you thought something to the effect of:

> "That was an excellent point. (Of course it was. :-) I can understand how that would help me grow. My situation would make a great illustration in another one of Gerry's books. I'll drop him a note about it."

and/or:

"I'm not too sure I agree with that point. (Oops, sorry; another fault revealed.) I'm going to write to Gerry and let him know how I see the situation. Maybe he will grow from MY ideas!"

The vast majority of people I have interviewed agree that we all have thoughts of nice things to do for others and ideas to help others grow and improve. Yet, in just about every case, we fail to follow through on our good intentions. It can be as simple as remembering an old friend and thinking "I should drop them a note." or "I'll look up their number and give them a call."

Make it a habit to praise others.

One way to get better at giving praise is to set specific goals for follow-through. Stop by the post office and buy 12 pre-stamped postcards. Mark your calendar for a particular day of the month, say the second Tuesday, first Monday, last Friday, or whatever. Do this for every month for the next year. (Better yet, buy 52 postcards and make this a weekly habit.) Give your most positive enthusiasm to your special "Praise Others Day."

On these days, look for special actions done by others, and listen for positive thoughts you have about people in your life. When a strong feeling hits, get out the postcard, write a short note and send it to the person you have in mind.

You will be surprised at the results, because both the recipient and you will learn something from the experience. Sending the card will make a great day for *both* of you!

Here are some examples of times to spontaneously grab a postcard:

- You hear an "oldie but goodie" on the radio and it reminds you of a friend from years ago. Send a note and tell them of your remembrance. Maybe something like "Gone from the chart, but not from heart!"

- You notice a co-worker taking time to re-explain a process to a new employee.

- You feel a strong memory about a relative or friend and think how special they are to you.

- You remember a few paragraphs ago you felt strongly about sending the author a note.

- You read in the paper about a person doing good works in the community.

Do it now, before it is too late.

None of us know when our time on this earth will be finished, and virtually everyone has experienced wishing they had said what they felt before it was too late. And even worse, is the loss others feel wondering what the departed may have left unsaid, and unwritten. Obviously, this "we never know when we're going to go" applies to everyone: family, friends, co-workers and self.

When it comes to co-workers, there are special ways you can acknowledge them through different levels of thank you notes. Your efforts on their behalf will have significant, positive impact on both their perspective of you and their recognition on the job.

Six levels of acknowledgement.

There are six levels of recognition and encouragement you can deliver. Each level contains all the benefits of previous levels plus increased impact on the perception of other people about the person being thanked and increased impact on the recipient's perception about you.

First level.

This thank you is the simple spoken word. It is intended to be heard by only the recipient. It is more than the "thank you" we use in polite day-to-day conversation, because it contains specific reasons and descriptions of the action prompting you to seek them out for this special statement of appreciation. Result? Usually a smile, a nod of appreciation and a "thank you" for the "thank you."

Second level.

Taking the time to write an electronic note says you are further convinced the effort of the recipient is worth mentioning. The electronic note provides a record that can be printed and saved by the receiver. An accumulation of such notes builds one's self-worth by becoming an affirmation of "goodness" from the perception of others.

Third Level.

Hand-written notes are becoming a rarity as computers and electronic mail take over the world of written communication. A note or letter, when hand-written (especially when done on personalized stationery or specially purchased thank you card) tells the receiver your feelings were strong enough to take the extra effort to write it by hand. At this level, a hand-written note has greater value than one keyed into a computer. This is because one must take extra time for planning what to say (text editing is much more difficult once the words are on the paper) and for making the note neat and readable.

Fourth Level.

At this stage, it is necessary to start making other people aware of your perception about the person being thanked. A Level One thank you can be said in the presence of the recipient's peers and superiors. Carefully timed opportunities can generate additional acknowledgements from others in response to what you say. Level Two notes can be electronically copied to the receiver's boss, letting the receiver know you are willing to let the boss know your appreciation. It is not likely you would copy someone else on a Level Three note, but do consider a separate note sent to the superior, indicating you, in fact, did send a note to the person being thanked.

Fifth Level.

At this level you become a direct advocate for the person being acknowledged. This is done by sending a detailed and descriptive written, typed or electronic note to the supervisor or manager of the person being complimented and a copy to the person being complimented.

Two things result from this effort. One, the supervisor becomes aware of the situation and the performance and can apply appropriate recognition if justified. Two, the person being complimented realizes your commitment and willingness to involve their management in a positive way.

Sixth Level.

The most powerful acknowledgement you can send is when you elect to describe your perceptions to the second level management (or higher) of the recipient of the compliment. Copies to lower level management are necessary to keep them aware that the exchange occurred. At this level, it is most powerful not to copy the person being complimented. If they know there is extra observation being done, they may feel pressure to behave in ways other than their normal pattern of behavior. Allowing their natural habits and personality to continue will provide further evidence of the validity of your observations. At this level there is a definite implication you believe their behavior needs recognition, reward or acknowledgement by management.

The Added Bonus.

Throughout all these processes there is also a growth for the sender of the "thank you." The effort necessary to compose a well worded statement provides the sender with new experiences in writing, helps them in their sensitivity to the work situation and puts their name in front of higher management. While certainly the intent of such thank you notes is not to benefit the sender, many times that is exactly what happens. Managers and supervisors appreciate the extra effort put into such notes and your observations provide the management team with a fresh perspective unavailable otherwise.

It all comes down to this:

> **You gain considerable respect and appreciation when you are willing to praise others.**

When delivered with sincerity and moderation, flattery and praise is a powerful business communication tool. I recall a phrase, source unknown, summing it up well. It reminds us that everyone enjoys a compliment.

> **"Flattery will get you everywhere —
> Keep talking!"**

A sure-fire way to obtain flattery for yourself from people who really care is to . . .

16. Have a Support Network.

The ability to personally and professionally grow is accelerated when you have the following seven advisors in your support network:

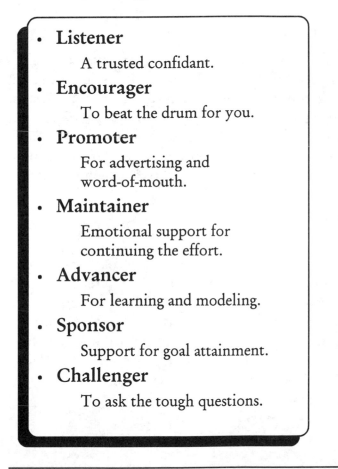

- **Listener**
  A trusted confidant.
- **Encourager**
  To beat the drum for you.
- **Promoter**
  For advertising and word-of-mouth.
- **Maintainer**
  Emotional support for continuing the effort.
- **Advancer**
  For learning and modeling.
- **Sponsor**
  Support for goal attainment.
- **Challenger**
  To ask the tough questions.

1. The Listener.

This is a trusted confidant who will take time to listen to your plans and goals. Advice is not given by this person. They simply serve as a sounding board. Through skilled rephrasing of your statements and personal, intimate conversation, they help you fully develop and solidify your ideas and goals. The more the Listener listens, the better you sound.

2. The Encourager.

This person beats the drum for you and gives positive support in whatever you decide to set out to accomplish, learn or create. Advice, if given at all, takes on the form of suggestions for improvements and ways to obtain even more encouragement. Encouragers give you a constant positive boost to your ego and your sense of accomplishment.

3. The Promoter.

This person almost causes you embarrassment! Through word-of-mouth references and advertisement of your ideas, progress and determination, they consistently tell everyone how you are changing and improving, and how you are the best person for the job at hand. Promoters give you a sense of pride about your progress.

4. The Maintainer.

Ongoing emotional support is given by this person, especially when you are discouraged or have suffered a setback. In the good times, they help you preserve the momentum with congratulations and pats on the back to continue the effort. Maintainers help you want to continue your quest.

5. The Advancer.

This is a special person who introduces you to advanced concepts, helps you learn new subjects and explains how to apply these ideas in your life. They serve as a role model by demonstrating the new behaviors you need to master in order to progress beyond what you currently consider as your potential. Part of your drive comes from wanting to be more like the Advancer.

6. The Sponsor.

This person, directly or indirectly, frees up time for you and gives physical and economic support for your goal attainment. They also endorse your efforts by influencing the people who have control of the assets you may need. This person helps you with methods for scheduling your time and securing resources, and suggests other approaches to accomplish more with less effort and energy. Sponsors help you know you are able to accomplish your goals in a timely manner.

7. The Challenger.

This is the person who is willing to ask the tough questions and to demand rational, well thought out answers. They ask "How?", "Why?" and "So What?" questions. They make certain you are prepared to deal with your strongest antagonists. Challengers give you confidence by verifying you are ready to explain your goals and rationally deal with your critics.

The seven functions described above, and the abilities necessary to deliver them, may be found in one very capable person, or you may have to find several different individuals to fill the diverse roles. Seek out people who have helped others to mature and succeed. These people are called mentors.

Mentors.

Mentors are people who enjoy seeing other people excel. They will not be jealous, envious or angry when you succeed, even beyond them. Mentors succeed through the success of those they help.

Mentors see your potential long before you realize or accept that you have it. Many times, they will seek you out and will give you tremendous support without your asking. Sometimes a mentor will be helping you grow without your realization that they are doing so.

Your value to the business, your co-workers and your self will go up considerably simply by the association you have with your mentors. Your self-confidence will increase. The growth goals you set for yourself will be achieved with greater ease and certainty because of the resource you have in the experiences, successes and perspectives of your mentors.

> **Having a network of mentors enriches both your potential and its attainment.**

Chances are very good that your mentors will tell you about the tremendous strides you will make when you . . .

---

17. Volunteer for "People" Things.

On the surface, getting involved in social and celebration events, kick-off and recognition meetings, picnics, holiday and seasonal gatherings may seem to be just extra work. Experiences of others may suggest the additional contribution goes unrewarded, and if immediate reward is the objective, then it is probably best to avoid this suggestion.

Doing extra work to improve the morale of the people in the business is a long-term investment in your relationship to the business and the people who run the business. The ideas presented in this chapter are usable even if you work for a very small company with only a handful of employees. The growth obtained in the implementation of these ideas also can be achieved by applying them to religious, community, civic and professional organizations.

Why would you want to take on extra work with little direct and immediate reward?

- To learn.
- To try out new ideas.
- To grow.
- To mature.

To Learn.

Working with a group of people who have done the event before will be an experience full of war stories of what did and did not work in the past. People repeating service on committees such as the ones mentioned, are probably there for one of three reasons: they enjoy doing this kind of work, they were ordered to join the committee or they recognize the long-term rewards of such work.

The people on these committees apply procedures similar to those used in running the business. To hold a successful event, there must be establishment of goals and objectives. There are planning and brainstorming meetings, budgets and deadlines to meet, work to be assigned, research to be done and measurements to be put in place. It is kind of like running a very small business with a predetermined life span.

Events like those mentioned allow members of the committee to do many business processes in a short period of time. It is a great way to observe and learn how other people do this kind of work. It is an opportunity to teach others the business processes you know.

To try out new ideas.

Celebration and special events are people intensive. People are the focus of the event, its content, and its execution. For rave reviews, these events require the generation of creative ways to get and hold the attention of the people attending.

There are ample opportunities during the planning process to apply creative thinking techniques. Usually, a higher than normal acceptance level will be present. This greater level of tolerance allows for more bizarre and off-the-wall thinking than is normally allowed in the more restrained situations of the "real" business world. The people who have worked together on these unique projects will have a special ability to tolerate and appreciate the more dramatic creative ideas that previously had been rejected back on the job.

Trying new ideas also includes learning about the allowable limits of the business, especially when dealing with humor. Humor plays a large role during special events. How far can skits, roasts, sarcasm and parody go when dealing with the reputation of the business, management, executives and clients? The inside information learned in the design and writing phase of special events gives tremendous insights about the nature of key people and functions of the company.

Finally, as you try out new ideas, others will begin to know you better and on a more personal basis. If you discover their reactions to you and your ideas are positive, you may soon find them encouraging you to expand your participation and influence in the business. Likewise, a firm rejection to your efforts may also reflect some conditions of your business relationships of which you were not aware. In either case, you have learned more about what to do and what not to do back on the job.

To Grow.

Serving on committees and supporting special events provides you with growth that cannot be obtained elsewhere. Where else can you "let your hair down" and test the waters about your personal perceptions of the business? Where else can there be direct contact with higher levels of management as they check on the progress of the upcoming event? When you serve on these projects, leadership opportunities come much more rapidly than might be the case on job-oriented committees. Once your leadership is established on the event committee, do not be surprised to see business leadership opportunities offered to you back on the job.

Those who volunteer for the additional work are looked at by outsiders as somewhat out-of-the-ordinary. Your performance on the special event committee is one thing, and the very fact you are there is quite another. By voluntarily being involved, you send a signal to others that you are concerned with the success of both the event and the business. Others are in the background, lost in the shadows, but you have stepped forward. Simple observation says you are different. Not necessarily better or worse, but different. Well used opportunities send a strong message that you want to stand out. Such behavior is a mark of a potential leader.

Repetition is an extremely powerful way to establish recognition. Keeping your name and face in front of the key people in your organization will be to your advantage when decisions are being made about people. Whether regarding promotion, increases and rewards or reassignment, downsizing and termination, being a familiar face and name will put you in a more positive light since people know you, your skills and your attitude beyond just those used on the day-to-day job.

To Mature.

Maturing is defined as "the emergence of personal and behavioral characteristics through growth processes"[22] and "having attained a final or desired state."[22] Maturing through event participation comes after multiple efforts and when consistent results are produced. Let's say your organization has four special events every year. If, over a five year period, 18 of the 20 events held are considered successes and two are considered "bombs," hopefully, you have been associated with more successes than failures. If you participate only once or twice, you have a greater likelihood to hit one of the not so good performances.

With multiple experiences, you will find yourself maturing in the processes of special events and people will associate your participation with the successful ones. Primarily, the successes will

---

[22] Webster's Ninth New Collegiate Dictionary

---

increase for you because you will be maturing both in the processes of event coordination and in your ability to work with people. Positive indicators of your success include other's comments directly to you about your contribution and growth, and your own positive self-evaluation of your abilities and maturity.

Other rewards are numerous: business contacts made, growth in your ability to organize, schedule and coordinate people, realization of different aspects of the personalities of the people you work with and for, and self-satisfaction knowing you helped bring an enjoyable event to the business.

> **Participating in "people" events will give you personal and professional development experience otherwise unavailable.**

The easiest and most beneficial way to get involved with people events is to . . .

18. *Be an Active Citizen.*

No matter what your political, religious or social beliefs, there are organizations who need your help. By getting involved you share your abilities and experience with others and you receive back new abilities and experiences otherwise unobtainable.

Volunteers are needed.

In every community there are numerous organizations, committees and councils who depend on volunteer contributions of time and energy. Lions Clubs, Kiwanis, Knights of Columbus, the Rotary, YMCA, YWCA, Chambers of Commerce, libraries, Boys and Girls Clubs, Scouting, Big Sister/Brother programs, churches, temples, assemblies, food banks, missions . . . the list goes on and on (If I missed your favorite, sorry. :-) Every one of these and other fine organizations offer you powerful learning opportunities for personal and social growth.

When you join a civic, social or religious organization and volunteer your time and service, there will be at least five primary benefits.

1. Your interpersonal abilities are nurtured.

You will learn how to interact with people who have no knowledge of your technical abilities. In many cases your technical expertise is of no value to the organization. Because of this, the interactions you will have with the people and processes of the organization will be invaluable to you. Through these interactions you can learn how to better communicate your ideas, your hopes and your dreams for the organization you have chosen to join. If you are able to successfully communicate with the variety of personalities involved in this new organization, doesn't it stand to reason you will get better at interacting with the myriad of personalities at work?

2. You get a dose of non-technical reality.

These types of organizations, especially those dealing with serious social issues, can be instrumental in helping you put your day-to-day technology into perspective. What is really important? Increasing the transaction capacity of a computer system or decreasing the number of hungry people in your community? Getting a technical problem diagnosed and resolved or finding a home and job for a single parent family? Meeting a proposal deadline or establishing a crisis hotline for prevention of suicide and domestic violence?

3. You gain *ASK*.

You and your business can gain from newly learned methods of information recording and distribution within a social project. In turn, social projects may gain from your technical expertise as they design systems to capture, disseminate and use information and services. It is a win-win environment.

4. You will establish a useful network.

There will always be people from other businesses and walks of life participating with you on these community projects. You may meet a person who would delight in being a mentor in your support network. You can learn from business associates who may have been faced with the same business challenges you face today. The products and services of your business may be needed by one of your community peers. The result is, your community activity produces real business leads and opportunities for your company. Networking with other professionals leads to business opportunities not available in any other way.

5. You receive the personal satisfaction of contributing.

Above all else, you will have the personal satisfaction of knowing your ***ASK*** are contributing to the betterment of the greater community. It also stands to reason that the sometimes negative image of highly technical people would be quickly replaced by a whole new perspective about the technology when you are seen in the light of community activities and contributions..

> **If we all committed just 1% of our time to a worthwhile civic activity, imagine what a better world this would be.**

Regardless of the organizations you join and serve, you will find the only way for a person to excel in this rapidly changing world is to . . .

19. Embrace Change.

Today is certainly different than yesterday and tomorrow will no doubt be different than today. Change is inevitable. It is said, change is the only constant in the universe. Change is one experience in life everyone has in common.

When change is offered to us, or thrust upon us, for the most part, we resist the change. It is comfortable to leave things the way they have always been. This "comfort zone" of our existence gives us protection from the rest of the world. It also prevents us from perceiving the opportunities seen only from a different viewpoint.

When things change, our perception lags behind. Our experience holds the patterns we use to find definition, understanding and comprehension. Using the past as a model, we perceive things as they always were. These models in life are called paradigms. Paradigms are the patterns of the way we perceive the world. Change is the changing or shifting of one or more paradigms. In other words we must be aware that:

Shifts Happen!

Paradigms and perception.

A paradigm is "an example serving as a model; pattern."[23] Generally, paradigms are patterns held by groups of people. As individuals, we have our own patterns of reality. These patterns are just as powerful as any paradigm held by a larger group.

Another word for these personal patterns of reality is perception.

Perception: "immediate or intuitive recognition."[23]

Recognition: "the identification of something as having been previously seen, heard, known, etc."[23]

By substituting the definition of recognition inside the definition of perception, **perception** then becomes "immediate or intuitive identification of something previously seen, heard or known."

We perceive the world through that which we have seen, heard and known — our experience. Things outside our experience have a difficult time becoming part of our acceptable reality because they don't fit, don't look right, don't sound right or don't make sense to us. In other words, these new experiences (changes) being offered do not match the model (paradigm) of the way things have been.

---

[23] The Random House Dictionary of the English Language.

> **When your patterns of reality do not match the patterns of others, conflict occurs.**

A paradigm can be so strong it will filter away anything not matching the known pattern. We are blind to the opportunities a new paradigm offers. When our paradigms change, our filters change and we are allowed to perceive something that was imperceptible in the past. The result of a paradigm shift is to see things as never before; to become aware of the obvious.

Most people get through the "shift" of change by processing the new in terms of the old. They filter, modify, distort and reshape the new in an attempt to get it to match the patterns they <u>can</u> conceive. Seems to me, all of this is a great deal of work. Wouldn't it be easier to accept change, embrace it and get on with it? Obviously, from what we have learned, it is easier to say it than to do it. There are some techniques to help:

Listen — Review — Restate

Listen to others and your own self-talk for statements suggesting a change (shift) in the paradigm (filter). There are three primary ways people will indicate a perception has changed:

- "Oh, I *see* your point now! I must have been *blind* not to *see* what you were *showing* me."
- "Hmmm, I *hear* you now! I must have been *deaf* not to have *heard* what you were *saying* to me."
- "Ah, I *understand* you now! I must have been *numb* not to *sense* what you were *offering* to me."

Review the information previously filtered away by the old paradigm whenever a shift is detected through one of the above or similar statements. This also applies when your internal thoughts are similar to the examples above. It is wise to go back several minutes, even hours or days to re-examine the issues, because up to the point the perception shifted, the information was not getting through — literally!

Restate the elements of the change after the review. Do all the parties involved understand each other? Get agreement of the common perception (the new pattern or paradigm) before moving on.

Assuming your thinking has now been changed through what you have learned in this chapter, the following will help summarize (**review**) what has been covered:

> The weather is a great example of constant change. No matter where you travel in the world, the locals pride themselves in the fact their weather is unpredictable. They will tell you, "If you don't like the weather, just wait a few minutes, it will change." The same is true of many things in life, "If you don't like the way things are, wait a while, they will change, and maybe you'll like things the new way."
>
> Sadly, the corollary is also true, "If you like the way things are, wait a while, things will change and you might not like the change."
>
> What many people have learned during their lives is this: **most of the time we do not want things to change**. We are accustomed to the way things are and to change things puts us into stressful situations as we explore the unknown territory of the "new way."

Change is around whether we like it or not; therefore, it is beneficial to take full advantage of change and the opportunities within the change.

> **Those who handle change
> with greater patience,
> more understanding,
> and less resistance
> have a greater possibility of
> succeeding as a result of the change.**

Controlling unwanted change.

When presented with a new way of doing something, if you feel the change is not for the best, you are faced with one of three possible paths.

1. **Change it.** If you have the power and authority to change things for the better, then do so!

2. **Influence it.** If you are not able to change things yourself, but are able to *influence* those who have the power and authority to change things, then get on with influencing them!

3. **Embrace it.** If you cannot change things yourself and you cannot influence those in authority, then get on with the change and stop resisting the inevitable! Resisting inevitable change is futile by definition.

> People who expend energy resisting change, fall far behind the people who channel their energy into accepting the change and leading it.

Why technologists resist change.

Technical people tend to strongly resist change to the technology of their expertise. This is because they know (very well) the way things are. Any proposed change threatens the very thing that makes them an expert. Allowing change to take place puts the technologist in the vulnerable position of not knowing the way things are. There is the added fear that there may be others (peers, strangers, competitors) who know the intricacies of the new way better than the technologist does. Knowing more, the "others" may become more valuable than the technologist who knows and believes in the current way.

Success strategies for any change.

There are three things to do to be successful regarding change. First, become aware that

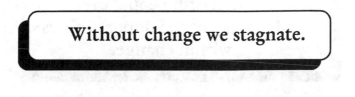

> Without change we stagnate.

There once was a billionaire who decided to build a castle. To add to its charm a moat was built around the castle. It did not take long for the moat to become filled with algae and slime. It created quite a stink. The design was flawed. There was no provision to allow fresh water in and old water out. The moat become stagnant and the castle became unlivable.

A better design would have been to frequently drain and refill the moat. Unfortunately, that also kills all the good little frogs and fishes in the moat.

The best design of all allows the living creatures in the moat to survive, by continuously supplying fresh water and draining off the old.

> **Successful people frequently let fresh ideas in and stale ideas out.**

Second, become an advocate of change rather than an adversary. Learn all you can about the changes and the opportunities within it. Accelerate past the resistors and even past the instigators of the change.

> **Successful people take advantage of the opportunities within change.**

Third, come to the realization that the only way to improve things is to change them.

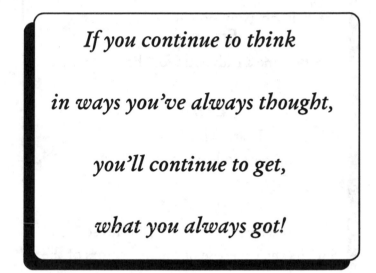

If you continue to think

in ways you've always thought,

you'll continue to get,

what you always got!

> **Strategies for dealing
> successfully with
> inevitable change.**
>
> **Embrace it.**
> Become an advocate for the change.
>
> **Learn it.**
> Learn what is needed.
> Seek to learn even more.
>
> **Lead it!**
> Accelerate past those who resist.
> Surpass the expertise of the instigators of the
> change.

Even in the most difficult and unwanted changes
there is always opportunity to . . .

20. Find Something Good in Everything.

> **Things are neither good or bad, but thinking makes it so.**
> **— William Shakespeare**

People like to be around people who think positive. I have noticed people tend to avoid me when I am in one of my "everything is bad" moods. Gee, why is that? Why would people rather be around a positive thinking, upbeat person? Could it be, misery makes lousy company?

Good versus bad.

How do you approach everyday situations? Do you look for the good in everything? Or, is it easier to find something wrong with everything you encounter?

Most technologists tend to be concerned about every single detail of their technical world. They know very well just one thing going wrong can set up an entire chain of events resulting in a great big problem blossoming where only a tiny seed of variation was planted. Technical people are on the watch for any little thing going wrong. This is good because that is one of the things technologists are paid to do! The bad thing about this sensitivity to looking out for what can go wrong, is that it influences us in our more general thinking about non-technical situations, other people, and life in general.

It is my observation that the deeper one delves into technology, the more cynical one becomes about the number of bad things that can happen. We insist every rule be followed, all blanks be filled in, and no one is to touch the controls except the technical expert! This intense insistence is due to our fear of a circumstance occurring that is beyond our ability to handle it. If we cannot handle it, such an event threatens our credibility as a systems, procedures or technology expert. Thus, we seek to find every possible negative condition as a way to prevent a disaster occurring in the system.

Unfortunately, this pursuit of the negatives becomes a fine-tuned skill and a vicious habit carried over into other parts of life. This problem is resolved when we more logically approach each situation we face. (Logic is another great skill of highly technical people, so let's use it to find a way to counteract the potential negative attitudes our other abilities have instilled in us.)

Approaching a situation on our job (or in life) with a "What can go wrong?" questioning habit will help us discover the risks and potential failures we face. When we turn the logic around and ask "What can go right?" we may discover previously unknown opportunities and possibilities to excel hidden in the situation.

Right versus wrong.

One way to keep a positive flow in your thinking is to force yourself to find two things right every time you find something wrong. For example, how are things at work? If you think of something negative, can you instantly find two positive things? How is the president of the U.S. doing? For every negative, find two positives. How about the commute to and from work? Your parents? Your children? The boss? Today's news? The weather? Can you find two good things about each situation?

For example: Pick a subject you tend to think negatively about. Complete this short exercise:

"Two negative things about _____ are:

1. _____

2. _____

. . . and what you have written is absolutely correct, for your experience forms your thinking patterns (paradigms) and "thinking makes it so."

The challenge is to now find two positive thoughts for every negative thought above. Concentrate, and find things with the same level of intensity, but indicating a positive disposition about the same subject. Complete the following statement:

"Four positive things about _____ are:

1. _____

2. _____

3. _____

4. _____

. . . and what you have written is absolutely correct, for your experience forms your thinking patterns (paradigms) and "thinking makes it so."

_____

If we concentrate on the positives, we will begin to strengthen our "positive thinking." The habit of stopping to seek the good in every situation will not negate your ability to find the technical glitches in your systems and procedures. What it will do is open the door to new positive thinking and positive perspectives about people, places and things in your life. As a bonus, along the way you may discover new perspectives leading to the need for newer and better technical solutions, and, after all, that is *also* what technical professionals are paid to do!

Risk versus opportunity.

When presented with a situation involving risk, people tend to imagine the worst outcome immediately. One way to give yourself a reality check and open the door to some breakthrough thinking is to shift the focus to the opportunities at hand.

Example: You know the system design for project X is flawed. The boss thinks it's great because the boss designed it. You are concerned there is risk in standing up and speaking out against the design. Ask yourself: "What is the risk here?" A typical thought pattern follows:

"If I say something . . .
- The boss will get mad,
- I'll probably get fired,
- I'll lose my house,
- My family will leave me,
- I'll be living on the street, homeless,
- I'll get some terrible disease,
- I'll die, and
- They'll throw me in an unmarked grave!"

All this over one comment?

Ask yourself, "What is the opportunity here?" Possible result:
- The boss commends you on standing up for what you believe in.
- The boss admits you are right.
- You get a promotion for your sharp thinking.
- You save project X from failure.
- The company performance skyrockets.
- Your stock becomes worth millions.
- You become independently wealthy.
- You retire to a life of leisure!

All this over one comment?

Both scenarios are probably unlikely. The important thing is, you may want to rethink each situation with a reality check. What is one probable negative outcome? Project X fails. What is one probable positive outcome? Project X is a success.

What _is_ the risk?
  A small confrontation on design.
  A bruised ego.
  A short talk with the boss.

What _is_ the opportunity?
  To save everyone a lot of grief.
  To take a responsible leadership role.
  To learn.
  To influence.
  To grow.

"Yeah, but . . ."

I remember when I was a child, around our house if someone put the word "but" at the end of a phrase, everyone else would say "Yeah, but . . . " in anticipation of the negative thing about to be said. It didn't always go over very well with the speaker, but ("Yeah, but . . .") it sure made the point! (I guess it would have been better said as — It didn't go over very well with the speaker, _and_ it sure made the point!)

One way to avoid the negatives is to cease using the word "but." The word "but" when properly used shows an exception for clarification. "Last winter was very mild, but for the storm in late January." In other words, the winter was mild with one exception. Another example is the Shakespeare quote at the beginning of this chapter.

"Yeah, and . . ."

Unfortunately, we tend to misuse the word "but" and say things like "I really like your new hair cut, but it's a style I didn't expect." In this case the "but" negates the statement that you "like the haircut." In other words, the statement is saying, "I do not like your new haircut because it is an unexpected style." This example is an ideal case for substituting of the word "and" for "but." It makes a world of difference: "I really like your new haircut, and it is a style I didn't expect." Not only does the use of "and" turn the statement into a truthful positive, it also builds a positive relationship.

The "Yeah" in "Yeah, but" is easily assigned a sarcastic overtone. Being careful to not be sarcastic with the "Yeah" in "Yeah, and" will most likely cause the phrase to be thought of as a supportive statement ("me, too!"), which it is!

Thumper, the cute little bunny in the Disney movie Bambi said, "If you can't say anything nice, don't say anything at all." This is an excellent philosophy for projecting a positive attitude around people. However, (Yeah, but. . .) keeping things in balance also means avoiding being naive about the negative things that can happen with systems and technology.

When dealing with my auto mechanic, I would rather know <u>now</u> that the car will eventually stop running if I do not replace a bad wire, belt or hose rather than waiting for the failure and then asking "Why didn't you tell me so?" The attitude used by the mechanic to tell me the bad news is where the Thumper principle comes in to play. Give the information, and be nice!

Would I rather hear "That pile of junk you call a car is headed for trouble again!" or "There is something I'd like to tell you about your car to prevent a future failure." In either case I'm going to be out $152.87. In one case, it is a negative nagging expense and in the other case it is a positive preventative investment.

"What I Like . . ."

Here is a technique to apply to both yourself and others when the thoughts and comments take on a negative tone:

Whenever someone tells you what they don't like about an idea or situation, simply ask the question "Well, what do you like about it?" Be sure to put the vocal emphasis on the word "like" rather than "do." Let's observe this technique in action:

Pat: "I hate it when I have to come in an hour early to do the payroll!"

Chris: "Well, what **do** you like about coming in an hour early to do the payroll?"

Pat: "Hmmm, well, I like the fact that I beat most of the traffic . . .
I get to go home an hour early (or) I get an hour overtime (or) I get to be appreciated . . .
I'm certain I'll get *my* paycheck . . .
I don't have to work on project X for a couple hours . . .
It's nice and quite in the office . . .
I know the coffee will be good because I made it . . ."

Chris: "OK, OK! Enough! That's more than I expected!"

Pat: "But I like this approach! What do you like about getting more than you expected?"

Chris: "Hmmm, I like the variety of options, the creativity, the interaction, the new thoughts, the ease of doing it, the . . ."

Get the idea? This technique can be used in virtually any situation. Even the most negative event can take on a new, positive perspective if we are practiced at finding the good in it.

The most important thing you can do with your new attitude of "finding the good in everything" is to find the good in **you.** The more good you find within you the easier it will be to . . .

21. Believe in Yourself.

Remember the journaling you were encouraged to do in Chapter 4? Once the journaling habit is established, your journals become a wonderful source of self-worth. By reading your journals, especially when several years have passed, you will find much to be proud of and will find great insight and inspiration.

Reading your words and your perspectives about life will help you more strongly believe in yourself and in your self-worth. While reading, you may find things you would like to change about yourself. These discoveries have great positive value as well, because they remind you of what you want to believe about yourself. Your belief becomes focused on what you can be, what you can achieve, and what your future potential may be.

In reading your journals you will also discover many things you like about yourself. These revelations are heartwarming, endorsing, energizing and empowering. Only you have your particular perspective. Your view of the world is unique. Because of this unique perspective, as you learn more of it, you will find yourself generating even more unique and powerful ideas for your future. Such thoughts will rapidly build positive belief in yourself.

Be not easily frustrated.

Believing in yourself also means making a conscious effort to avoid frustration. I was once told, "Gerry, be not easily frustrated and you will achieve much." My response was, "Be not easily frustrated? Easy for you to say!" (Obviously, I was frustrated by the statement. :-)

This is a challenging concept, somewhat like "Be spontaneous." To be spontaneous, one simply needs to react to the stimulus presented. There is little one can do to **be** spontaneous, it cannot be forced. Neither can one force themselves to "**be not** easily frustrated." Frustration just happens, spontaneously! Right?

The best strategy is to keep a level of consciousness allowing you to be aware of when you are trapped in the hold of frustration. When you observe frustration occurring, take a deep breath, count to 10 (or "one-zero" :-). In just a few seconds you can provide yourself the much needed refocusing and redirection of the energy being used in processing the frustration.

Consciously channeling your frustration into energy for positive creative thinking, will help you break out of the grip of frustration. As you take regular doses of positive self-talk, you will be well on your way to a healthy attitude and a strong sense of self-confidence.

You may find yourself trapped in old habits and thought patterns. Negative self-talk may sound something like:

"You can't do that! It will never work! What have you got to be confident about? You'll never be able to change!"

This is the time to remember what you learned in Chapter 6 — "Fake It 'Til You Make It!" (FITYMI) Give yourself a boost, a shot in the arm, the benefit of the doubt and turn your negative self-talk into positive belief in yourself and your untapped potential.

To help rid yourself of old patterns of negative self-talk, try this approach:

> # Listen for negative self-talk, then negate it!

I call this the "double negative" technique. It is based on simple mathematics. In mathematics, two negatives multiplied together makes a positive. This is true about negative thinking also! It is extremely easy to implement "negative, negative thinking" and is also very enjoyable. The next time you hear your inner voice saying something negative, give it a blast of its own negativity!

"What do you mean I can't do that? Who says? It will **never** work? **Never?**

Give me a break! **You're** the real jerk here! You **never** think positive! Matter of fact, I think it is **you** that does not have any self-confidence! I can change anything I want, including **YOU** and I'm going to do that right **NOW!**"

Give negative self-talk a dose of its own medicine. If you have been good at negative self-talk in the past, this should be easy. Factor in a negative thought about the negative thought and Presto! — you have a positive result!

"I'm going to give this a try. A new approach will give me a fresh perspective. I have successfully changed myself in the past, I can do so again. My ability to change is obvious, for I am a much better person today than I was yesterday!"

When you believe in your ability to do something competently, even if it is a FITYMI pass, do that something with confidence and take full responsibility for the results. In the rare case where there is a failure, your willingness to be fully responsible will help you further build belief in yourself. How? By coming to the realization that you are solely responsible for your actions and other people cannot limit your potential to learn and grow.

> **Taking full responsibility for your actions removes the limits put on you by others.**

The final thought on believing in your self is this: just like success, excellence and achievement, ambition is self-generating and self-fulfilling.

> **The more ambitious you are, the more ambitious you are!**

All you need to do is start. The rest will take care of itself, because if you believe in yourself, you have eliminated your worst critic.

Part IV

Time:
The Final Element of
Success

Reallocating Time Means Reducing Stress.

There is more to life than your job and the technology associated with it.

Life is much more than the technology so swiftly passing by everyone, expert or not. Life dominated by work is simply that — work. When you are gone the people at work will miss you — for a few moments, then the work and the processes will continue as if you were never there. When you are gone, the people in your life, your friends and family, will miss you much more than the people at work do. Your family may never get over the loss of the miracle called "you." If they do adjust, it will most certainly take them a lot longer than it will take those at work.

What is really important?
Do you recall the death of a co-worker? It is a sad event, no doubt. Did the business or co-workers dwell on it over a long period of time? Did it mean the collapse of the business? Not likely.

And, if it did, I suggest it was a rare exception. Are you that exceptional on the job? Are any of us?

Do you recall the loss of a family member or close friend? Was the event forgotten quickly? Not likely. Was there ever the threat of collapse of the family unit? Frequently, yes. What will the single parent do? How will the finances work out with only a single income? What can be done to overcome the loss of one who is so deeply loved and needed as a companion? I suggest this overwhelming sense of loss is a common occurrence. Are you an exception to the love of family and friends? Are any of us?

If your work is all-consuming, you miss the opportunity to contribute to your family and friends outside your job. When you are gone, neither work nor family can have more of what you brought.

> **Your employer counts on your *ASK* to get *some of the work* done.**
>
> **Your family depends on your *ASK* to get *all of the love* done.**

Corny, but true.

If only . . .

When you are gone, if you were overly consumed by work in such a way as to weaken the relationship with your family, friends and community, could it be your family might not be as affected by your passing? Wouldn't that be the ultimate tragedy — not to be missed by anyone?

As far as I have heard, there have been very few people, if any, who on their deathbed have said "Gee, I wish I had spent more time at work." The classic remorse, when time is clearly drawing to a close, is "If only I had spent more time with those I love; if only I had done the more important things; if only I had found my dream and lived it; if only I had used my time more wisely; if only I had it to do over again I would do it a lot different."

The endless pursuit.

Unless one is born into wealth, employment is necessary to produce the income to live a reasonably comfortable life; therefore, making time for yourself and family is not necessarily easy. Consider, however, the trap excessive work gets us into — the eternal pursuit of income to pay the debt of possessions.

I've talked to many people of various income levels, and it seems no matter how much a person earns, they remain behind financially, as if there is some reward in pursuing "things." Debt builds until we are focused only on paying the debt. If only we would wise up and pursue relationships! While still there is an endless chase, the journey is the reward itself. Instead of building debt, we accumulate credit for a life lived with much more value and self-worth.

Since it is not easy, we must study ways to make it happen with the least amount of stress and friction.

> ## Time is the one great equalizer of us all.

Reallocating time.

We all have a fixed amount of time. For most of our lives, we have been programmed to believe we can somehow "save" time. Advertisers want us to believe that by using their products and services we can save a few minutes here and save a few minutes there and let them accumulate as in a bank account. Then, at some other time, we can withdraw our "saved" time and use it all at once. It doesn't work that way. All we can do is rearrange and reapportion the fixed amount of time given us.

The way we allocate our time is a key factor in our level of contentment and comfort in life. Two different people, with the same jobs, relationships and time can have substantially different results, depending on how they apportion and use their time.

When it comes to the allocation of our time, first and foremost are the choices we make. When we give in to the pressures of the job, we make a choice. Many times we believe if we do not give all our available time do get the job done, we will lose our job. That may be true some of the time. But, if it is true all of the time, why would anyone in their right mind stay in such a job, year after year? If the work load is so great and unyielding, what does that say about the philosophy of the organization? Where will it all lead? — to early burn-out, stress, unhealthiness and loss of the very thing one is working to achieve — success and personal happiness.

If the suggestions made in this book are followed, time is made available for reallocation. For example:

- **Educating yourself:** Knowing how to do something better than your peers keeps you from becoming bogged down with the extra time needed to get the work done the less educated way.

- **Delegation:** Accepting the premise that when others are able to handle the job without your attention to every detail, time is made available for reallocation.

- **Respect:** Recognizing when someone else is wiser than you, more experienced, or at least a step ahead of you, learn from them! What they know will help you get your job done better and faster.

- **Communication:** Becoming a master at asking questions, giving more than others do, and selling well will increase the quality of information exchanges and will reduce the time needed to do it.

If you value your time, and follow through with a commitment to make better use of your time, you will find many ways to reallocate it. How does this happen? It happens as a result of simply realizing there is a fixed amount of time available to you. While this seems like a very simple and even naive concept, there are few people who have accepted they have a limited amount of time. When the realization hits, you are much more aware of where you are wasting time.

By following through on a sincere desire to reallocate the time you have, you will seek and find numerous ways to accomplish your goals. You will use the ideas in this book and the ideas from many other sources. There will be new significance to old time saving tips due to your new awareness of what you are searching for.

> **I seem to have misplaced my stress.
> If you find it, you can keep it.**

What if, while you have been reading this book, your boss got hit by a truck? So what? Well, certainly one would not wish a disaster upon another human being, not even to one's enemy or competition. If a person you work for is incapacitated, there will no doubt be an impact on the business and on the amount of work to be done and maybe even on the amount of responsibility you must take to keep the business flowing.

What if a loved one, your spouse, child, parent or friend, were the one seriously injured in this imaginary situation? The first situation pales in comparison. The loss of a co-worker is insignificant compared to loss of one who is really important in this life.

Take all of this a step farther — what if your office burned to the ground? (I know, it will mean you will finally get organized! :-) What if your home burned to the ground? Is there any reasonable comparison? What is really important?

So, **where is the stress?** At work?

NO!

> ## The real stress is in your personal life.

There is nothing more important on this earth than your religious beliefs, your family, friends, and the service of others. (If we disagree on this point, I am very sad for your spirit.)

When we spend extra time at work, handling what we are falsely led to believe is stress, we actually are taking away the precious time needed to handle the situations and relationships of our personal life and our home life where the greatest stress resides. It stands to reason we should free up some of the over-dedicated time we spend at work to deal with and resolve the real stress-producing factors of our personal relationships outside the job.

Reallocate your time and your stress levels will change. Find the combination you need for the best relationships at home. You will never regret it.

You will never regret it because . . .

Reducing Stress Means a Happier Life.

Jeff Smith, the Frugal Gourmet, recently said on one of his TV shows, "Life is too short for fast food." That thought stuck with me, and I feel his philosophical statement captures what this book is all about.

We go through life looking for fast fixes. When we are hungry, there are drive-through restaurants. We can't wait for someone else to pump our gas; so pump-your-own is the rule. We have fast lanes and high speed merging lanes, express checkouts and express trains, electronic funds transfer, remote controls, power door locks and power windows, credit cards for groceries and court fines, dial-up data bases, technical support and catalog orders, electronic telephone solicitation and automatic pet feeders! Where does it stop?

Fast food and all the other things we demand in an instant come to be only through competent, professional technologists behind the scenes. Sadly, in this fast-paced, high-tech world we begin to believe that technology and systems can solve all our problems. We forget about taking time for others, and we forget to take time for ourselves.

> **Stress lowers and happiness rises when *you* take time for *you*.**

Life is too short for fast food. Life is too short for fast fixes. Take time for yourself and others. The time spent with them is a gourmet meal you will remember; always, and in all ways.

Re-programming the human technology.

We have to be smart and skilled to know how to use the wonderful brain we were given. All the technology in the world will pass away and be replaced by something cheaper, better, and faster. Every system ever designed will be outdated someday. The only constant in all of the technology is human technology; the human being. Maybe that is the problem. We look at ourselves as a constant, rather than the ultimate and most valuable re-programmable variable.

By directing just a little more of our time and energy to developing the human side of ourselves, we stand to gain a much more productive balance in our lives. The human factor is much like the attitude element in *ASK* presented back in Chapter 1 where I said "Attitude is not everything, but it might be the only thing."

> ## The human side of life is *not* everything! But, it might be the *only* thing!

While there are times when it appears technology may save the day all by itself, the human element is always present. Technology without the consideration of people serves only other technology.

By fine tuning the technology of our people abilities, we get more from our human side. And, as in all systems, by getting more from the same resource we may solve previously unsolvable problems; we may find answers to unanswerable questions. In the long run, we may find that personal satisfaction and fulfillment is found in filling the gaps between people.

Human beings? Human becomings!

Ricky Dawson, a fellow motivational speaker, says. "The most difficult 18 inches in life is getting what is in your head to move into your heart." His message inspires me to summarize this book in this way:

> ## Your technology is in your head.
> ## Your potential is in your heart.

The technical side of your life is in your brain. The people side of your life is in your heart. Whatever you do with it and whatever you achieve with it is in your mind. What is your state of mind?

For the greatest success in life you must listen to other people and observe what they communicate about their feelings. You need to project a positive attitude if you expect people to listen to you and let you show them how things are done. While your thinking still resides in your head, the influence of your heart gives you the purpose and reason why you do the things you do.

> ## The formula for success:
> ## Be competent with technology
> ## and compassionate with people.

As specialists and technologists we often spend a disproportionate amount of time and energy in our heads, dealing with systems, procedures and technology. When we do this, we become a pain in the neck to the others who do not have the luxury of our technical expertise. Worse yet is when we bypass the potential of our heart and take the pain in the neck south about twenty-four inches and become a down right pain in the a _ _! (rear :-)

Both pains can be relieved with a generous dose of learning and growing the *ASK* of a well rounded professional. Applying the *ASK* of technology **and** the *ASK* of people, ensures that our greatest potential can be realized, and that we have the most value to our company, community, friends, family and self.

As an adult, if you **will** yourself to grow and to change it **will** happen. Your will begins by getting your attitude right. With the proper attitudes you can engage the skills you possess which are the manifestations of your knowledge. As you apply your knowledge you begin to define your purpose and your purpose gives you your motivation. Your motivation reaffirms and empowers your will.

- ♦ **Will begins with attitude.**
- ♦ **Attitude powers skill.**
- ♦ **Skill applies knowledge.**
- ♦ **Knowledge defines purpose.**
- ♦ **Purpose gives motivation.**
- ♦ **Motivation powers will.**

It is a beautiful, endless cycle; the closest thing known to a perpetual motion machine. How is your machine powered? Where does your will lead you?

Certainly, being a well balanced and successful professional is a life-long challenge. This balance is similar to the pursuit of excellence, quality and perfection. It is a journey and not a destination. Enjoy the trip.

On your road to success and happiness will be highs and lows of both technical discoveries and people discoveries. For a very few, the greatest reward will be in the arena of technology. The experience of those who have been around for a while indicates, for the vast majority, the fondest memories will come from the people side of life.

> **Dost thou love life? Then do not squander time, for that is the stuff life is made of.**
> **— Benjamin Franklin**

What time is it?
Look at your watch. No matter what time you say it is, that time is past. It was true — for an instant — and then it was gone. There is only one time to be concerned with. Now.

What time is it? It is now. Now is the time to reallocate your energies into the attitudes, skills and knowledge of a successful professional person. Not tomorrow, or next week or after the current project is completed. The time is now. The sooner you begin a conscious balancing of your people abilities and your technical abilities the sooner you will realize the results, rewards and self-satisfaction of a more enjoyable career and a more enjoyable life.

The time is now. The only way you will grow and become a greater contributor to yourself and others is to begin now. The following to-do list is one used by every successful person, no matter what their job or goal in life. It is up to you what you do with it and what you do with the rest of your life.

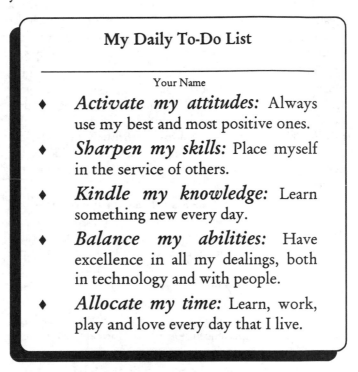

My Daily To-Do List

_____
Your Name

♦ *Activate my attitudes:* Always use my best and most positive ones.

♦ *Sharpen my skills:* Place myself in the service of others.

♦ *Kindle my knowledge:* Learn something new every day.

♦ *Balance my abilities:* Have excellence in all my dealings, both in technology and with people.

♦ *Allocate my time:* Learn, work, play and love every day that I live.

May you achieve every success you desire, accomplish every goal you set and realize the full satisfaction of your potential. Godspeed, my friend. Thank you for letting me be part of your journey.

About the author.

Gerry Reid is a professional speaker, educator, consultant and author. His vision is "to provide people with usable information and positive inspiration to take full responsibility for bettering their own lives and the lives of others."

Thirty years with GM and IBM provides Gerry with a wealth of business experience. His background includes positions in computer technology, management, marketing, product development, education and service organizations.

Gerry delivers motivational speeches, training workshops and educational seminars that are content-rich and his delivery is natural, friendly and engaging. His expertise is in building and mastering integrity, responsibility, ownership and follow-through. His offerings include numerous topics dealing with strategies for achieving personal and professional success, and enhancing the perceived value of technology.

Personally, Gerry Reid is a blend of philosopher and pragmatist, with an emphasis on discovering better ways to do things without destroying the fundamentals that created past successes. He is down-to-earth and looking to a future filled with unlimited dreams, ideas and potential.

For over twenty-four years Gerry has been involved in motivating, training and educating people. He has more than sixteen years as a seasoned speaker, educator and consultant. Internationally experienced, Gerry has spoken or taught in 38 states and 13 countries.

ASK for Success! is Gerry's first book.

Appendix A.
Characteristics Survey

The following is a summarization of 1024 responses to the question "What is one thing you demand in people you work with?" Technical professionals and technical managers participated attending *Techies are People, Too! 17 Bits to Set On or Off for Success.* The survey was taken 12 times from August, 1993 through May 1994. Audiences were at Common (2 meetings), Share, the Enterprise Expo, and local and regional computer user group meetings in Charlotte, Dallas, Dodge City Nassau, Milwaukee and Minneapolis (2), and at one IBM Availability Specialists conference. Presented in alphabetical order within ranking:

88 listen
77 honest/truthful
50 humor/fun/laughter
50 respect/respectful
46 friendly/amiable/personable/outgoing/smile/
             warmth/smiles/pleasant
44 clear non-technical language/speaking
36 open/open-minded
35 integrity/credibility/trust/trustworthy
34 attitude, positive/helpful
33 team work, team player,
             team oriented, partner
29 willing, desire to learn/listen/work/change/
             adapt, flexibility/acceptance of change
27 communication
27 dedication/loyalty/commitment/conscientious
21 cooperation
19 care/caring/concern about others/work/
             people/company
19 understanding/understand people
18 knowledge/smarts/brains/expertise/

intelligent/common sense
16 courtesy/polite/kindness/considerate
16 technical ability/aptitude/expertise/
    skills/proficiency
15 compassion/love/sensitivity
15 dependability/reliability
15 empathy/emphasize
15 patience
14 competence
14 people skills/relationship/relate to others
12 works hard/ best effort
10 accountability/ownership/follow-up
10 fairness/treat others as equals/not superior
9 professionalism
8 accountable/responsible
8 brevity/concise
6 acceptance, get along with others
6 inquiring mind/inquisitive/curiosity
6 responsive/responsiveness
5 perception/see big picture/wider view/
    others viewpoint
4 appearance/attire/hygiene
4 clear vision/objectives/focus
4 complete/completeness/completed staff work
4 enthusiasm
4 logical
4 self-motivation/starter
4 sincere/sincerity/genuine
3 balance
3 confidence
3 humility
3 sharing
3 writing skills
2 accuracy
2 adaptability/adjust
2 buy-in
2 consistent
2 creativity
2 eye contact
2 interest in other people
2 outside interests
2 perseverance/persistence
2 problem solver
2 self respect
2 simplicity
2 support
2 understand the business/functions
1 "we can" attitude
1 ambition
1 analysis
1 apathetic
1 approachability
1 aptitude
1 awareness that other things exist
1 better physical shape
1 build rapport
1 business atmosphere
1 comfortable environment
1 common ground or interest
1 compatibility
1 compromise

1 concentration
1 decisiveness
1 don't jump to solution
1 don't demand
1 don't talk down to users
1 draw our peoples' needs
1 drive
1 egoless programming
1 engage and breakdown easy
1 engagement
1 enjoy everyday
1 entertaining
1 ethical
1 excellence
1 excitement
1 expense
1 experience with variety of situations
1 family
1 feedback
1 feelings
1 fit in with other techies
1 forgiving sense
1 fortitude
1 forward
1 getting a point across
1 graciousness
1 gerry loves pam for infinity
1 happy with themselves
1 human relationship balance
1 human attributes
1 increased vocabulary
1 initiative
1 interesting
1 interpret user needs
1 know what you do know,
                what you don't know, don't BS
1 know your audience
1 learning new things quickly
1 light-hearted
1 like it
1 lots of energy
1 make the other person seem important
1 mediate conflict
1 no weasels
1 not a prima donna,
                do not put down others who know less
1 non-competitive
1 non-offensive
1 not condescending
1 objective
1 observing
1 on the same level
1 others perspective can get into user's shoes
1 outspoken
1 pacing
1 perfection
1 pocket protector
1 political ability
1 practical application of knowledge and skills
1 put yourself in their place
1 quality

1 quick comprehension
1 recognition
1 relaxing attribute
1 restate at various levels of expression
1 result-oriented
1 save time, don't reinvent wheel
1 sense of silly
1 set context for users before going into detail
1 shoe on the other foot,
            look from user standpoint
1 spirit, excellent
1 summarizing
1 sympathize
1 take the time
1 technology is only a tool
1 thank you babe i love you
1 thick skin
1 think of the options
1 thoroughness
1 time
1 tolerance
1 twenty-four-hour mentality
1 understand each others functions
1 undivided attention
1 value people as much as hardware
1 vision
1 visualize solutions
1 want to help
1 why ask why
1 work on yourself; cannot change others
1 work ethics
1 works well with others

Appendix B. Subject Journaling Ideas

If you are stuck trying to think of something to journal about, try this technique, just for fun. Take any dictionary, turn to the page number represented by the last three digits of your home telephone number (call this number X). Starting in the upper left corner of the left page and go past the number of words represented by your age (call this number Y). The next word (or one nearby with special appeal) is the word you should use for your first subject journal. Start by copying down the entire definition.

If you don't like the word found there, then take the number of pages in your dictionary, subtract X from it (if negative, ignore the minus sign), and go to that page. Start at the bottom right of the right hand page and count Y words backwards. Try the next word, or any other appealing word you have seen as your subject. If you are still not satisfied or want to have multiple subject journals, repeat this entire process substituting the following variables for X and Y:

X		Y
Last (or first) three digits of your birth year.		Your waist size in inches (or centimeters).
Square root of your zip code (or area code).	Number of windows in your house (or office).	
Number of dollars spent last week on groceries (or beer)		Months since your last vacation (or physical exam)
First (or last) three digits of your social security number.		Number of steps (or light switches) from your front door to the bath(or bed)room.
Last (or first) three digits of your address.	at work.	Number of floors (or elevators)

Twelve (of the thirty-six possible) words this methodology created for me were: interjectory, migraine, hypodermic, mutualism, bug out, tanked, euthanasia, profound, chevy, start-ship, cedar chest, and stream-flow. Several of them have very strong appeal to me: mutualism, euthanasia, chevy, star-ship and stream-flow. See ya' later. Gotta' start journaling!

ASK for Success!

21 Ways to Enhance Your Image and Maximize Your Potential

ASK for Success! is a perfect presentation gift for a friend, or in recognition for a job well done by an associate. This form entitles you to special pricing.

Title:	Price	Qty	Total
ASK for Success!	_____	___	_____

Quantity discounts:

    1 book - $16.95

    2 books - $15.95 each

    3 books - $14.95 each

    4 or more - 13.95 each

Shipping and Handling $2.50 each ___ _____

Check, money order, Visa, Mastercard TOTAL _____

Card Number_____

Expiration Date_____

Signature_____

Special discounts available for larger quantities, bookstores, resellers and fund raising events. Write for details.

Name_____

Address_____

City _____

State or Province _____

Phone/Fax _____

☐ Check here for additional information about
   Gerry Reid Speaking services.

Send order to:

Gerry Reid
c/o Edwin Thomas & Sons, Publishers
4333 Essex Court, Suite 103
Flower Mound, Texas 75028

Attention order department:
   ASK for Success!

Thank you for your order!